TO RAP AN

To Rap an Asshole

A Narrative Rhyme to Challenge You

Newton Phillip

JANUS PUBLISHING COMPANY
London, England

First published in Great Britain 1996
by Janus Publishing Company
Edinburgh House, 19 Nassau Street
London W1N 7RE

Copyright © Newton Phillip 1996

British Library Cataloguing-in-Publication Data.
A catalogue record for this book is available
from the British Library.

ISBN 1 86756 260 7

All rights reserved. No part of this publication
may be reproduced, stored in a retrieval system or
transmitted in any form or by any means, electronic,
mechanical, photocopying, recording or otherwise,
without the prior permission of the publisher.

The right of Newton Phillip to be identified as the author of
this work has been asserted by him in accordance with the Copyright
Designs and Patents Act 1988.

Cover design Harold King

Printed & bound in England by
Watkiss Studios Limited, Biggleswade, Bedfordshire

Contents

Who Needs Wisdom	1
The Wisdom of a Single Tongue	20
Rights and Wrongs	31
Environmental Influences	50
Law and Order	66
Fear and Beliefs	76
Truth and Lies	91
Offender and Offended	102
Love, Like, Hate, Dislike	112
Sleeping Demons	126
Five Bridges to Cross	135
Natural Segregation	147
A Sharing Need	154
The Folly of Your Ways	163

Who Needs Wisdom? (Saggezza)

Man has lived a thousand years . . .
Never! Okay for ten thousand years.
What! You must be joking; but no,
science has proclaimed that it is so.
Supported with evidence and some hard facts,
They dug up from the traces of human tracks,
uncovered from beneath the earth
And with their secrets intact, which time has wrote.
Man has lived for a million years,
The exact count, well, who really cares?

And during that period,
he has developed numerous skills,
Carried by the wagon of time,
down through the ages.
His experiences he took with him to his grave,
to soothe his damning decomposition.
His knowledge and his understanding,
to his fellow man he wills
When his life confronts its termination.

But what has he done with his wisdom?
Is it with him in his grave to be found?
Or returned to the wilderness where it belongs?
Or is it that he had none to give?
And when he departed, he left you to live,
to find your own wisdom.

For wisdom is that which he rarely seeks,
And so with wisdom he seldom meets.

He just lives a life full of wrath,
Wet dreams and troubles are his food for thought,
Vanity and folly is the web in which he is caught.
His pride is in the victories of the battles he fought.
And all without wisdom.

Wisdom – man dared to ask the nature of its being.
Are you in a shape and form
or a spirit in the wilderness drifting?
Are you in flesh as a body warms,
or just space among galaxies?
Are you a gas or a liquid?
Or are you something solid?
A meteorite or a star
or something unknown from a distance afar?

What art thou, oh wisdom?
so few men have ever asked.
And where art thou, oh wisdom,
could you be, but right before me passed?
Are you the food for thought?
Or a necessity that cannot be bought?
Or the light the darkness sought?
Like a torch that swallows up the night.
Or a fire that voraciously devours?
Are you visible or invisible?
With a reflection or a shadow?
Are you with scent high or with scent low?
Or just a sound without an echo?
A virus in the air,
Blown like a dust from here to there.

Are you athletic or academic,
of the physical or spiritual,
a genius of geniuses, or just a scholar,
an architect of ideas, or a creator of thoughts?
To man's inspirations, to him you brought.

Are you a wish or some burning desire
eating at the core of man's brain.
The cuckoo in a cloud whistling aloud,
no need for man's ears to strain.
Are you something useful or something useless,
A companion or a pest,
A foe or a friend,
Trustworthy to the end?
Or a genie enslaved to do man's bidding whenever he willed?

Wisdom who are you? What are you? Where are you?
man has dared to ask.
Are you among the trees
Floating in the breeze,
Or in the air dripping with the rain
Into a canal and down a drain,
Through my roof and onto my bed.
And onto the pillow beneath my head.
Or in the toilet where I sit,
Or among them toiling in the pit.
In society among us all,
Scribbled in graffiti on a wall?
Or are you some distance afar
In a galaxy suited for a star?
Or are you right here under my cheek
Playing your little game of hide and seek?

Wisdom, oh wisdom, to you man pleads
Your inspiration is what he needs.
Tell him quickly where shall you meet.
Where shall he follow, just you name the street?
Where must he search, for where art thou?
Hidden like a shadow behind a cloud.
You have no face, you've got no voice.
Are you without shape and form,
Is there no place where you belong,

Or a womb from where you were born?
Or are you from the sea,
or from deep beneath the ground?

Who needs you wisdom?
Why do you hide from us all?
And hardly answer whenever we call.
Could you not hear and could you not see,
That man's need for you is a matter of urgency?
Why do you play so hard to get?
Has no one ever caught you yet?
Wisdom, who needs you anyway? We can surely get by.
There is no need for you to emerge from the place where
 you hide.
And as day follows day, to forget you we must
And get on with life in faith and trust.

Noble kings and wretched paupers,
they were all born alike,
From woman's womb pushed out,
during the day and during the night.
To become part of a family,
extending roots from its natural source,
Given life, inherited
from the rhythm of the act of intercourse.
And from the climax of that caress a babe was born
To fulfil a task in providence from that day on.

Burdened with a destiny of rights and wrongs,
You inherited a place on the family tree,
Although not yet knowing what you would be.
You inherited their name,
the human web of family ties
And their traditional values,
whether they are foolish or whether they are wise.
You inherited most things,
all with sins or with blessings

In an environment that teaches,
and where you learn all things.

Given food and drink, clothing, shelter and warmth,
Love and affection, sometimes with an obsession,
or in moods of vexation,
But all with love.
An irritating crying in wet nappies torn
That wrapped an itching bottom
in the shit that feels so warm.

You crawled along smiling
whenever there was nothing wrong,
And halted without a warning,
sometimes just to listen to a sound.

You stood upright, to walk and then to run.
In nude artistic, and without a blush, absolutely no fuss,
You are just having a bit of fun.
And not yet knowing that you were growing,
Not yet knowing what is right, from what is wrong.

So you played with fire, not knowing the danger,
You fell off some height and broke a finger,
Sickness struck, and with the peril of some bad luck,
Crying all night, and as stubborn as ever.
Always there is something the matter.

You don't want that and you don't want this.
During the night it's on your bed where you piss.
Afraid of the dark, loves a horse and cart,
Hate water, no, just hate having a bath.
You don't want a doctor;
you wouldn't stay with a stranger,
And no one knows what the hell is the matter.

Causing trouble both day and night

Kings and paupers alike.
Innocent creatures to overcome their plight,
Crying and crawling from the darkness into light.
With arms stretched outwards,
as though reaching for a bike
To peddle on your journey,
from your cradle to the things in your sight.

On your journey you began,
from your cradle to your grave,
Led onto the road, and often you are told
just how to behave.
You learned first who is Mummy
and then who is Daddy,
And to say thank you with a smile,
when they change your nappy.
You learned to crawl and then to walk,
And in their language you learned to talk.

You learned to enquire sometimes so curiously,
About safety and danger,
good and bad behaviour,
and often painfully.
You learned not to touch
the things you ought not.
With a hammer it is a blow,
and with a knife it is a cut.
You learned what is to eat and what is to drink,
And to write with a pen you must fill it with ink.

You learned to wash when you were dirty,
although you would have preferred to remain so.
And that you would be punished when you were naughty,
from yourself you cannot hide – no place to go.

You learned to change your clothes and to comb your hair,
To hide your private parts when others were there.

You learned to brush your teeth,
always to look smart and neat –
the things your parents do is because they care.

You learned that there is a God
and there is a Devil,
For good there is reward
and punishment for evil.
You learned your way to school
to church and the market place.
Some things are acceptable
and others a disgrace.

You learned to count and to read and write,
You can spell your name and you can fly a kite.
You learned the art of saying no
when you really meant yes
And to sort things out
when they were in a mess.

You learned the skill in a trade,
to become a master with tools.
In mathematical problems you applied the rules.
You learned French and geography, medicine and history,
You acquired knowledge and obtained a degree.

You can sing well and play the piano,
Tell fortunes and predict a volcano.
You can dance and perform in a sexy romance,
Climb a mountain, and in deep waters you can swim.

You can land on the moon and even on Mars,
Or just travel around the world in flashy fast cars.
You can heal the sick and rebuild an ugly face,
And mend a broken heart without a mark or a trace.

You learned to fly high up in the sky,

And down the river you go, in the boat you row.
There is so much to learn,
despite how much you have known,
And yet they called you dumb,
when so much you have learned,
Whether you sit upon an ass or upon a throne.

You learned to dress in fancy style.
Although you hate her guts,
you greeted her with a smile.
You told an ugly duckling that she was pretty,
You won her loving heart with your trickery.

And then you exploited her body
with your seductive fingers rude,
Till a climax in orgasm,
both locked in a position lewd.

You learned to love and you learned to hate.
You became a slave to the rules society makes.
You played in the game, a goal for you to score,
But what must you do? You don't know for sure.

You learned to live and don't want to die,
And yet you rush into battle not knowing why.
You learned that you must do what you are paid to do,
and often without a question raised.
And it really doesn't matter if they agreed with you,
you must follow the traditional ways.

You learned the game – survival of the fittest,
To slaughter or to lame those who are the weakest.
You learned and you learned more and more things,
That you are able to tell when it will snow,
or pissed down with rain.

And while all your learning was being done,

You often found some time for fun
In cuts and blisters and kisses from lovers
Overwhelming you with joy, or raging in tempers.

You learned whilst growing old graciously
There is always something to add to your memory.
Whether it be just a song,
Or the name of a new town,
Some scientific discovery,
Or the plans for a bank robbery.

A girlfriend's name,
The rules of a game,
An appointment with your doctor,
The school teacher or your solicitor.
The first time you made love wearing gloves.
Or whatever it is, even the answers for a quiz.
No matter what you do, never can you
fill your memory to its capacity.

But to learn is part of your whole life's functions,
You must learn to overcome all obstructions.
Whether you are a pauper or a king,
During your entire life you could be always learning
What you have to do, and what not to do.
Take it or leave it, the choice is with you.

Whatever your station your environment teaches well
The things you must learn between heaven and hell.
You started from a babe without a break or a spell,
You learned many different things to guide you well.

You grew up learning, and you learned to know
Of the traditional values you ought to follow.
And for all the things that you forget or remember,
Some questions you ask and some you never.
Without an understanding of why things are right or wrong,

Ignorance you choose, rather than to lose
the friends with whom you belong.

And during your lifetime of learning
there is always something more for you to know.
Your brain is stored with knowledge
and with a great deal of rubbish
that kept you on the go.
You learned from people
as well as from books,
And from the writings on the walls
that hang without hooks.
You learned from your environment
countless things influencing your mind,
That which guides your way of thinking,
be it ruthless, or be it kind.

You learned about the skies and the seas,
The earth and the heavens, and the universal mysteries.
You learned that wrong is sometimes right
and that right is sometimes wrong,
This depends upon the environment in which it belongs.
And amidst this confusion
you asked not why it is so
That a right becomes a wrong
in different places where you go.
Is this foolish, or is it wise?
But no one seems to know,
That the answer is in wisdom,
the path you must follow.

And in all your necessary learning,
gathering knowledge heap by heap,
There is something ever so willing,
but with it you never meet.
It is hardly even in your classrooms;
teachers don't mention its name,

So you never did get introduced,
yourself you can hardly blame.
By name it is called wisdom,
and it is with you on the street
Where you busily trample daily,
crushing it under your feet.

But then who needs to be wise?
Without wisdom you can survive.
Is it a passport to heaven;
can it save you from hell?
How much during your lifetime
does it help you to do well?

The pauper and the king alike,
One with poverty, and the other with might,
Both are in need of wisdom,
because both have battles to fight.
But neither ask the question,
"wisdom are you in sight?"
They both just carry on fighting,
the only way that they know is right.

But where do you find this wisdom?
Does anyone know where to look?
It is not given in your inheritance;
it is not written in a book.
Wisdom is all around you,
in front as well as behind,
But likewise you're a person in darkness,
eyes open, yet unable to find.
But if only you will zealously look,
and search deep down within your mind,
Then perhaps a little wisdom
upon you its light may shine.

You choose instead the common bed

that wisdom does not support.
A ruthless life, with aim to thrive,
even on a bed of iron wrought.
With your problems solved right or wrong,
like a magician and his trick,
Now it is here and then it is gone.
Your wits are never too quick.

During your life every day you meet
With friends and strangers upon the street.
And with your need to communicate
In opportune moments you do not hesitate.

And as you prepare to stroll along your weary path,
You are confronted with problems before you start.
So you continue to trot along
With survival your goal, and a will that is strong.

You learned many things,
you acquired knowledge and understanding,
skills and experience
and a talented prominence.

You are honoured and even distinguished with honorary
    titles.
You have been elegantly seated in high office,
And have obtained outstanding fame and greatness.

So said your king, your bishop, your emperor.
So said your president wherever he went.
And so said the peoples of every tongue,
So said they all, from wherever they belonged.

You are decorated and receive the most honorary trophy
For your requisite and ingenious discovery.
For your talented excellence
and your bravery in battle,

And for your courageous efforts
in some human struggle.

You acquired possessions of all the things desired under the sun.
Your arms stretched across the seas
to embrace lands from places far beyond.
You have power and a sea of wealth,
You are fit as a fiddle
and in very good health.

You have so much money
that you completely lose count,
And wherever you go,
you can have whatever you want.
You have powerful friends
and influence in the whole world all over.
So what more do you want
when you have an empire?
There's no need for wisdom,
money is your master.
It solves all your problems
in one way or the other.

You have so much
and always wanting more,
In a manner niggardy,
you exploit the poor.
You are pompous, boring and old,
Your face is freckled and your hair is grey,
Old age has claimed you in its conspicuous way.
You are charitable – no, uncharitable and miserable,
Some say that you are kind,
some say that you are ruthless.
A good man a bad man; who knows best?

You love the glory and the power,

And you want to keep them forever.
But you cannot cheat nature,
despite all your wealth.
You craved for happiness and peace of mind,
A good night's sleep, and a smile that is kind,
Perpetual good health you cannot find,
Despite all your wealth.

You make mistakes like everybody else,
Your fart stinks and your breath smells.
This is because you are not a god.
It is six feet under where you will fall,
When voice of nature whispers its call.
Despite all your wealth.

You may be foolish or you may be wise,
You lived in Eden or a fool's paradise.
You are just an asshole like all of us,
When nature calls, to obey you must.
Or you will be punished in such a way,
Shame and embarrassment you will display,
Despite all your wealth.

You have learned to communicate
as an essential necessity in your life,
And with this art you facilitate,
opinions end in strife.
But still there is no other way
For you to teach and educate
and to get along day by day
in the matters you negotiate.

And when you do communicate,
quite often just making friends,
It sometimes gets too intimate,
then nastily it frequently ends.

Consider all your arguments,
and then think why they all happened so,
Among families and friends,
neighbours and strangers,
institutions and nations, wherever you go.
The reasons and the source,
the roots and the cause of the arguing.
It is but just a difference of opinions
that started tempers rolling.

This difference of opinions is what you inherit,
A wide range of thoughts on a single subject.
Some foolish some wise,
and highly credited with merit,
But instead of exchanging opinions,
your own – you simply kept it.

Many arguments or quarrels measured big or small,
They are but a difference of opinions,
attached to them all.
You listened and you reasoned,
until you were hoarse or speechless,
Your ideas and opinions expressed at your best.
You shouted and you howled
and you beat on your desk,
And at the end of it all
everyone just left.
With nothing achieved, nothing gained.
Each held on to their own opinion without any change.
Whether it is foolish or whether it is wise,
who cares to know?
Wherever you are led,
you simply follow.

A difference of opinion often raises hell,
Among neighbours and strangers
and families as well,

Among kings and servants and bishops too,
Among nations and institutions
and the friends among you,
Among them honoured and among them disgraced,
And among them all, like fools in haste.

A difference of opinion is so well understood,
The aim and common goal, is to achieve some good.
To exchange your ideas with one another,
In prudent pursuit of a fruitful answer.
Views and opinions, opinions and views,
When inspired by wisdom, you cannot lose.

You said that you were wise,
and yet you lost a very good friend.
You freed yourself of your burden,
to enslave him to the end.
You cannot keep your secret,
so you passed it unto him
To hide it for you, deep under his skin.

But your friend, like yourself,
he is only human too,
And cannot bury your secret
in himself for you.
He must get it out of his system,
so someone he tells,
You learned of his betrayal,
and you let loose hell.

You never considered how hard he must have tried
To bury your secret
inside him to hide.
But just like you he had to puke it out,
And then to meet with your fury without a doubt.

Was that wise, a good friend to sacrifice

To set yourself free?
You enslaved your best friend with your secrecy.
Knowing only too well
that it was too hard for you to keep,
And yet you expected your friend,
Not a word of your secret to speak.

Are you foolish or are you wise?
That your very best friend you now despise?
And only because like you he was weak,
And your secret he failed to keep.

What a grave folly to have commit,
To be an asshole and a prick.
Whenever you are with secret that must be kept,
Share it with no one, until your death.
In this way it is safe to keep both your secret and your
    friend,
Until the last day when your life with death it collides and
    then finally end.

Within your environment you become a slave
To the influential forces that dictate your ways.
You learned from your parents,
what they learned is right.
Laugh at a joke and avoid a fight.
But as you move along to some other place,
To avoid a fight could be a disgrace.
The decisions you made influenced by pride
Are often foolish and seldom wise.
And when you choose the easy way
An asshole's game is what you play.

Just you tarry a little to think for a while,
Of the countless problems you faced during your life.
The decisions you made day after day,
In the home, on the streets, at work and at play.

And sometimes decisions are made for you,
Sometimes you excogitate what to do.
Sometimes you decide somewhat hastily
Not thinking of the consequences or the penalty.
But sometimes you act more cautiously,
Showing signs of worry about what may be.
And sometimes, although despondently,
yet in spirit amicably.
Sometimes a bit over anxious,
Wet in sweat, uneasy with tensions that make you nervous.
And sometimes although quite cool,
The decisions you made were those of a fool.

These decisions you made were numerous,
Some good, some bad, some dangerous.
And when they were made,
they were made to stick
Label you as a fool, an asshole or prick.

Consider the king Solomon, he was wise.
Two mothers came before him with tearful eyes.
And before him they staked their claim,
The child that each mothered was the same.

So in his wisdom unto them he said,
Let the child be divided,
be it living or dead.
And in his wisdom he had found
The rightful mother
to whom the child belonged.

To know wisdom you must understand yourself,
Not just in name and status,
though this too you must.
But yourself within yourself,
the shadow of your soul,
The spirit within you,

your inner dark hole.

You must discipline both your mind and your body
To the natural rhythm of peace and harmony.
You must rid yourself of all things evil,
And free yourself from the grips of the devil.
You must develop your observations
And deepen your meditations.
Be candid and open minded,
to embrace the virtue of wisdom.
You must be bold, merciful and merciless,
He who is wise is both kind and ruthless.

To be wise is to know when to agree and when to disagree.
What is right and what is wrong
is often a matter of controversy.
But in every right, as in every wrong,
There is a little corner
where a little wisdom can be found.
So search for it and get hold of it
and make yourself wise,
So that in this world you live in,
peace shall be your prize.

The Wisdom of a Single Tongue

Rights and wrongs in any language expressed,
In words or in deeds written or addressed.
For you to understand and to comply,
Hence language was formed for you to get by.

But what is a language, have you ever asked,
Or deep in your mind given it a thought?
This complex art of communicating,
For a single purpose, an understanding,
From man to man wherever he may be,
In the air or on land
or deep under the sea.
So for this reason language was formed.
Or was it created or was it invented
or did it just appear out from no where
Or through the passages of evolutionary processes,
was it constructed?
Or was it from the heavens by an angel brought
Thus to all mankind to be taught?
Or was it in a science discovered
From among the atoms of the horrors?
Or from an experiment it was found,
Blown out of the dust from under the ground.
Or in an explosion deep under the sea,
Or just from a desire to communicate with me?
Or was it just from the composition of sounds
Made from the wagging of the human tongue?

Yes correctly, it is an absolute necessity
Learned in your life very early.

' "So what is a language?" '
again only yourself to ask,
It is not a sandwich,
or you be a jackass.
For whatever you may think,
it is something far more than that,
It enables you to communicate;
it enables you to chat.

It is like music and it is beautiful,
It penetrates, although sometimes hurtful.
And yet it is all and simple a rattling of sounds
Given a specific meaning
for your understanding, whenever pronounced.

It is an art in letters formed
To represent the utterance of every sound.
Letters combined into the making of words,
Which are but a chain of sounds fluently composed.
Sounds into letters, and letters into words,
Words with meaning into sentences composed.

Words like a whirlwind in the atmosphere,
Conveying their messages to the human ear.
Through thin and thick and walls of brick,
Travelling words do reach you quick.

Words like a basket carrying messages
With their meaning intact they form languages.
And when a language is spoken that you understand,
Then communication is made;
it's like shaking hands.

But when a language is spoken
that you do not understand,
The sounds are so different;
it's like listening to nonsense.

Somewhat confusing, and without any meaning,
That is the language you don't understand.

But all the words in a language of whatever tongue,
They are all a rattling of sounds,
expressed in letters or characters, and combined into words
　　with a specific meaning.

And all words transmitting a meaning,
They must be arranged in order,
to awake an understanding.
When you arrange words randomly
You destroy their meaning completely
And you are left without a message
conveyed from you to me.

Take for instance the words
"I love you my darling,"
You grasp immediately their meaning.
You understood exactly what I said to you
Just as you did when I said "how do you do?"
Each word correctly following each other,
Conveying the message from one to another.
But now take the same words and rearrange them.
"Love I darling my you."
They lost their meaning
and they convey nonsense.
Sounds that you learn
become words that you understand,
The language of your environment,
the language of your land.

This language, a necessity to man,
In every corner, in shallow and deep water of every land.
Its only purpose is to communicate,
But when in a different tongue,
Then you will have to translate,

Sowing seeds of distrust, suspicion and hate.

Then why has man tongues so many,
Is it wise or even necessary
To say hello in so many ways
When you only really need a single phrase?

Is it foolish or is it wise
In so many tongues just to say that someone is nice?
Would it not be really better,
For everyone to understand one another?
Without ever feeling as a stranger,
Or a despised unwanted foreigner.
In different lands wherever you may go,
Be it Africa, France, Greece, or Mexico.

Would it not be better
to be able to communicate?
When in the same tongue
so many friends you can make.
Would you not embrace
a friendlier relationship
When with the same words you are understood
wherever you make a trip?
Would you not feel at ease, as if you are at home,
Instead of somewhat rejected and rather alone?

Then for what is the purpose of language,
If with your words you cannot communicate?
Is it for a necessity to separate,
with a frivolous desire to translate
In distrust, suspicion and contemptuous hate?
Will it be wise or will it be foolish,
To be a German, Brazilian, Chinese or Polish,
A Russian, Japanese, Iranian or English,
And in the same tongue to speak?

Will it be wise or will it be foolish
For a Greek to meet with an Irish,
An American to meet with a Spanish,
Or an Indian to meet with a Danish,
And in the same tongue to greet?

Will it be wise or will it be foolish
For every man to understand
His fellow man from every land?
Then why so many different sounds
Do you choose to confuse in foreign tongues,
And to listen through an interpreter?
When you are in love,
you want to speak with her.
In body language you embrace and caress,
And put your hands to grab hold of her tempting breasts.
You speak in action and not in words,
In a common act that draws you close.

But when with words you lose your tongue,
Because common words,
you simply have none.
So then you gaze upon the charms of her smile,
And feel yourself locked in a Paradise.
And at that moment you grasp hold of her hands,
The music in your heart is full of romance,
So then you spin her around in exotic dance.

Your emotions aroused and take a leap,
You pierce her heart and step on her feet.
You smile and she smiles,
but without words to speak,
When tongues are different,
hearts get close, but seldom meet.

And yet you want to be her friend.
How then are you to understand one another?

Your different tongue is a constant reminder
That you are different; you are a foreigner.
You can't converse or make a joke
Nor read the letter she recently wrote.
When your words are not hers
How do you expect to get very close?

And yet you want to be her friend,
Then you must be able to communicate,
To cement both hearts in relationship,
Like the sand and cement between two bricks.
You must be able to talk and laugh with her,
And not to share your words with an interpreter.

To tell her directly how you feel,
That love has punctured your heart
and for her it bleeds.
It is such words from you she loves to hear;
They gladden her heart,
as they knock at her ear.

But when your words she does not understand,
Then nothing you say
on her heart they will never land.
Such a friendship drifts swiftly to the end
Because nothing you say she can comprehend.
Then you lost your sweet heart,
you lost your girl,
Because she couldn't understand a single word.

Is it foolish or is it wise
to be a stranger when in a paradise?
Will it now seem to be foolish,
your own tongue to relinquish,
And to communicate with one another
In just one tongue in the world all over.

Or do you still prefer the many tongues
With their problems, their pros and cons?
Keeping man divided,
and when in foreign land to be stranded,
To feel rejected and alone
Among foreign tongues
which are not your own.

You go on holidays to different lands,
with intentions of having a smashing time.
But how could you achieve just that
When there is no one with whom you can chat?
You went to your hotel
And found that your room was not prepared.
So you made a complaint about that.
He nodded his head
as if he knew what you said,
and later he brought you a hat.

You don't know where to go, to see a show,
so someone you have to ask.
"I say! Do you speak English?"
"Ah yers, Engles,"
and he sends you to a football match.

You go in a restaurant to have a meal.
The menu they bring you,
you can never read.
You don't know what you ordered,
if it is meat or fish.
You hope only that when they bring it,
it is a tasty dish.

You can't call a taxi or ask for a whisky
without getting something else.
And when you ask, "Where is the loo?"
No-one understands you.

Nothing you can say ever helps.
You don't know what to do
For someone to understand you,
and your holidays are always a hell.

Would it not be nice to be alive,
In a world that has come to realise,
The common sense of having just one language?
One single tongue throughout every land,
With foreign man to communicate
Without interruptions to interpret,
And to have that feeling that you belong,
Making a joke and having fun
Everywhere and anywhere you go,
And with people you don't even know.

Would it be foolish or would it be wise,
Or would you be demoralised?
Would you lose your identity,
And be considered crazy?
Would some of your honour be lost
A damning curse to cause remorse?
Would you become inferior
With a complex or a chip on your shoulder?
Would you be named a jackass,
An asshole, a prick or an outcast?
Would you lose all your friends and your family
To be left alone, miserably?

Before a crowd you stood proudly to address,
With your charms and charisma
you intended to impress.
Then a silence reigned like the quiet of a peaceful sleep,
Everyone anxious to hear you speak.
And with your lingo that no-one understands,
You soon realised that you were in a foreign land.
And your persuasions never got through,

To grasp the hearts of those who loved you.

They listened to the patter of your foreign tongue,
Word after word just fell to the ground.
Everyone listened and everyone heard,
But no one understood a single word.
No-one agreed or disagreed,
And the leaflets you handed out,
they couldn't read.

So what was its purpose
when no one understood?
No one to say whether
your speech was bad or good.
How boring it had been.
Those foreign words you screamed.
A very good speech,
But no one did it reach.

Is it foolish or is it wise?
That wherever you may go you cannot speak,
You cannot converse with the people you meet.
You can't say hello, thank you or goodbye,
I say old chap, you better button up your fly.
You can't ask anybody where the hell to go,
Because they don't understand,
when it is not their lingo.

Then what should you do,
with everyone to communicate?
One tongue for mankind,
one tongue for human sake.
But then, could a single tongue be ever found?
Could intelligence play some part,
And help in persuading you
from your tongue to depart?
Is there no wisdom in man,

no understanding in him to be found?
To guide him to a start
in finding a single tongue.

Would it make any difference,
Or would it be an offence?
For every man to use the same words.
Whether he is from Switzerland or Japan,
or a remote corner of the globe.
Would it be some culture lost,
Or for the rest of your life you will be hoarse?
Or will you be hated with remorse
Because a single tongue you have found?

And now you have realised,
Whether you are foolish
or whether you are wise,
What language is all about.
It is just a rattling of sounds, represented by characters,
collected into words
And given a specific meaning,
which you store in your brain.

An artistic and an ingenious creation,
A requirement of every nation.
It obeys rules, to be perfect it must,
And although often misused,
its meaning never lost.
It contains power, both constructive and destructive,
And it is not affected by any natural or unnatural causes,
Such as a virus, or bacteria,
fire or water, good or bad weather.

Its powers are fierce,
Through the heart it can pierce.
It can also comfort and bring to you happiness,
When you are feeling depressed

and completely pissed
A kind word, a loving word,
a thoughtful word is a bliss.

With the power of love and the power of hate,
The power of language is like a roller skate.
It can take you speedily up,
and it can bring you speedily down,
And it can roll all over you
crushing you to the ground.

The rules in language to decide right and wrong
Are there to maintain uniformity,
within the traditional tongue.
To pronounce, to spell and to write.
In the creative form adopted,
It is but a language concocted,
And most of all,
it is the understanding of the wobbling of the human tongue.
Technology has drawn the whole world closer together,
And now, in a single tongue,
let us all communicate with one another.

Rights and Wrongs

From the moment you were born
and you learned to understand,
Dos and don'ts were an everyday command.
Don't do this and don't do that;
get on with this and please leave that.
All things decided,
they were either right or wrong.
From the heavens in the sky,
to hell under the ground.
Nothing was left forgotten outside the crystal ball,
Divided into rights and wrongs
were all things big and all things small.

Right and wrong, wrong and right,
It must be one or the other,
like the darkness and the light.
Never could they appear together,
never could day be night,
Never could anything be both wrong and right.

Right and wrong, wrong and right,
a haunting dilemma right through your life.
Imprisonment without a wall,
no electrified fence or bolted gates,
No guards or dogs or chains of metal plates.
And yet from right and wrong there is no escape.

Right and wrong as decreed from above,
In commandments given,
so that you can live in peace and in love.

Right and wrong in society too,
rules made by anyone to control what you do.
Bishops, teachers, politicians and employers,
Friends, strangers, parents and neighbours,
Anyone living and even dying too.
What is right and what is wrong,
is often decided for you.

Right and wrong in the manner you speak,
With words properly pronounced,
you sound posh and sleek.
Yes, right and wrong in the way you spell,
Is it night or nite, temporise or temporize?
You really couldn't tell.

Right and wrong in what you eat
For some it is only veg, others will have meat.
Chicken, beef or pork,
Or whatever beast they may have caught.
Don't eat this and don't eat that.
It gives you wrinkles or makes you fat,
An aching stomach or a heart attack.

And when it is alcohol you mustn't drink
Because it makes you drunk
and then you pissed in the sink.
You lose your senses and your self control,
And as a drunkard or an alcoholic,
you are well on the road.

Right and wrong in the manner you dress
You just not looking right,
though you do look a mess.
Your hairstyle, your blouse,
it's something about you,
Your skirt, your shirt,
the colour of your shoe.

Something is not right
and it just wouldn't do,
So get out of my sight
and return anew.

Rights and wrongs are ever so many
You want to help everybody
To solve the problems causing them worry.
But you don't know how to start
Because you got no horse, and you got no cart.
So you up and you steal a lorry,
A helping hand you must lend
To someone who is not a friend,
Only to make yourself sorry,
because of the worry,
Forced upon you at the end.

You hurried along to keep a date
Arriving early or sometimes late.
A business matter to attend
You pulled a fast one on a friend.
A car you steal, a house you break into,
Then someone else you framed
To let him take the blame.

Don't suck your finger,
you could suck your toe,
It is just a different flavour,
so why not have a go?
What does it matter?
It's just a joke,
Put in some chilli pepper
and piss in his coke.
He is just a foreigner,
He is not one of us,
Perhaps he will like it,
so what is all the fuss?

Right and wrong, wrong and right,
Some we impose and some we invite.
You want to love every man
And drop your knickers when you can?
Get to work for eight
Or do you prefer to be late?
Don't you dirty the street
Your rubbish you must keep.

Please be quiet
You can cause a riot.
Don't sit on that chair
Please move to over there.
This one is first class
And you are of low caste.
Take off your hat and put on your tie
You cannot come in here,
I don't know why.

You want to take the chance
And shit in your pants?
Put a bet on a horse
Or pay for intercourse?
A bank to rob
Or get yourself a job?
Spend your money on booze
Or gamble it and lose?
Then to take some drug
And drop off like a log.
To sleep on the street
Until with a policeman you meet.
Who takes the law in his hands
A corrupted policeman.
You make false arrest
Basic rights you suppressed,
With beatings and the rest.
Rights and wrongs.

You cover up crimes,
conceal documents and distort the truth,
An asshole you are,
a corrupted brute.
You protect criminals
from the wrath of justice,
And to ensure their protection
you even murdered the witness.

You bury inside you the evidence of murder,
Rape, larceny and brutal torture.
You would not speak the things you know
Because justice means imprisonment,
the place your son will go.
And with that guilt
you go to church,
You cannot find peace
wherever you search.
Nor from yourself can you hide,
Punishment will be yours,
as certain as that you'll die.
Yet it's someone else you are prepared to blame,
You cannot stand the gossip,
you cannot stand the shame.
Falsely you wear an honest name.

Pound foolish and penny wise
Both made a bet on telling lies.
Pound went to the station and confessed to a murder
That Penny committed last October.
Pound was arrested and convicted,
That was exactly what Penny wanted.

An eye for a tooth
a tooth for an eye
Do you want to swap
or do you want to die?

Your money or your life,
your life or your money,
You can have them both
and please do hurry.

Don't do that but you can do this.
Is it right or is it wrong?
It depends where you piss.
Shut your arse. Who wants to know?
The weather forecast, whether it is rain or snow.

You steal money just to spend it on booze,
You don't want to work,
that is the life you choose.
You rip people off
with the charms you use,
And like an ill wind passed,
you are on the move.

You took a stroll and you cajole,
You won her heart
so you think you are smart.
You got your screw
She became pregnant by you.
And now you are on the run,
Afraid of what you have done.
In rights and in wrongs.

But is it wrong to love for lust,
And right to love because you must?
You got yourself pregnant
and don't want the babe,
You took no precautions
whilst you were laid.
You both were so hot,
You enjoyed your fuck.
And now your responsibilities you want to evade.

You destroyed a life months before it was born,
You claimed that it is your right,
and that's the norm.
To have a screw
And then destroy the life in you,
Or to part from it after it is born.

You mustn't have sex outside marriage,
You can get yourself pregnant
and miss a carriage.
But if you must because of your lust,
Just remember that you can get AIDS
Without condoms if you screw.
Then, oh Lord, what will you do?
Put your hat on your face
and on your head your shoe.

You fell in love and then out again
In that abyss you cannot remain.
So you leave your smell on many a bed
To return one day from whence you came.

They said that you were one of those good doers
Who are always helping others.
You called yourself gay
when it should have been sad.
You have a sexual defect
and you claimed to be glad.
Always looking smart and respectable
With charms persuasive but dishonourable.
You entice a little boy
With the bait of a toy,
Then you screwed up his arse abominable.

You told a lie to save your daughter
Who was caught in mischievous behaviour.
But she was saved after tempers raged

And with one blaming the other.
Then you stripped her of her clothes
And beat her mercilessly with savage blows.

You cannot keep off the bottle
And when you are sober you just cannot settle,
And if advised you would not listen
To what is right and what is wrong.

You want your daughter to be like you
And nothing else will do.
So you give her no chance to find romance
Because her choice displeases you.
She must dress always in traditional clothes
And she must always agree with you.
She must sometimes lie
But never ask why,
As long as she did it for you.
And she must marry, although unhappy,
Only a Muslim, a Hindu or a Jew.

Rights and wrongs within the family –
You must not have sex until you are marry.
And if you do, I can only blame you.
Do not come in here with your big belly.

He is a lord, that rotten old sod
He raped the servant in his mansion.
But she lost the case and was disgraced.
They said it was her sexual provocation.

You told a lie and declared he was a spy,
just for thirty pieces of silver.
And then to save your arse you turned super grass,
So they found your body in a river.

You deceived with lies

And committed murder for a price,
Or sexually abused your own daughter.
A bank robbery, or assault and battery
Then you get yourself a smart lawyer,
Who convinced the jury to set you free,
So they all declared you were not guilty.
Right or wrong, wrong or right,
Questions requiring answers right now, during your life.

You often regretted most things you did,
And also regretted what you did not do.
Such are the decisions that you often make,
Right or wrong, affecting others the same as you.

You say so many things you do not mean,
And you mean so many things you do not say.
You do so many things you do not like,
And you like so many things you do not do.
Your sex crave, for instance, is that a romance?
You are a lesbian and you say that's okay.

You go to church for peace is what you search,
And you live a life of respect.
And yet you want her to die,
And the only reason why –
You cannot wait for the money you will get.
So you pretend to love her whilst having a go,
Slow poisoning her to her death.

You are such an asshole
Who can murder cold,
Even your mummy or your daddy.
And for what purpose?
You just felt that you must
Get control of their money.
So you killed for material gain
Causing destruction and pain.

Whether it is in a war,
Or within the walls around your door
It is someone's life that you claimed.
Is it that you are sick
Or are you just an asshole or a prick?
For such a sin to stain your name.
And then you are sorry for the wrongs you did
The moment that they are committed.
If only you will think instead of acting like a fool,
The consequences could have been prevented.

And yet the things that you did are often intentionally,
In your search for attention or sympathy.
And that what you did is usually crazy,
With spite, rage and hate, your potency.
So you hurt the ones that you love most dearly.
And then regret and be sorry.
For doing what you ought not to do,
And for not doing what you ought to do,
In rights and wrongs and in wrongs and rights.

And when you opened your mouth dirt came out
And someone innocent again got hurt.
But that which you had said
was not meant to spread,
It was only meant as a joke.

Don't blame me because you are lazy
I know that you are fat and have lots of money.
You like to eat well
And that is why you swell.
And you don't care a damn for anybody.

Don't drink and you mustn't smoke.
To earn a living you have to work.
So you get up every morning
Just to do the same thing,

Or else you could be broke.

You work many years and felt secured
In the same business where you were employed.
Then of a sudden you got the sack,
That sent your lifestyle right off track.
You did no wrong for what has been done,
And yet it is their right to knock you down.

You cannot come in here because you are black.
You sit over there, you are white.
You get in there, you are a Jew.
No one cares about you.
I am sorry, in here is only for men
Could you change your sex and come back then?

You cannot go in there; you are a foreigner,
And you cannot come in here; you are not a member.
You can or you cannot, do this or that;
It is either you are too tall, or your arse too fat.
And for your rights you often have to fight,
Or be refused for your entire life.
Wrong and right, right and wrong
Is there not a place where you belong?

A child needs a home with a family that's black.
A child needs a home with a family that's white.
A child needs a home with a family who can love him and
 teach him what is right.
Could white not love black
and black not love white,
To give a child a home
and bring him up right?
Is the colour of his skin
a main factor to decide,
Where love and care is to be given,
to a desperate child?

Is your decision right or is it wrong?
Has love and care got a colour,
in homes it cannot be found?

You are off to the country? Then take the car,
You cannot cycle that journey, it is too far.
So on your way you give a hitch-hiker a lift,
His gratitude, it was surprisingly swift.
He punched you in your face
Took your car off you and raced,
And ended up in a ditch
So you swore to kill the bitch.
Rights and wrongs, just a pocketful of rights and wrongs.

You killed animals for your pleasure,
To eat or just for fun,
for experiments or whatever.
Some in a sport ever so bloody
And during the cruelty, you bet your money
That one would savage the other.

You destroy nature just to create
A dangerous environment to populate.
You let your poison into the air
And you do not seem to even care
About the natural things that you need,
Such as clean air for you to breathe.
Your only concern is quick money to make
And when disaster strikes, then it is too late
For you to decide that it was wrong and not right.
So you lost your temper and found a rage.
You smashed things up in a craze
Only to feel sad after being mad,
And you ended up with a bill.

You persecuted some for not paying their debt,
when others' debt you write off.

And that, you say, is the only way,
to deal with such a cause.
Some got away when others must pay
to reduce the financial loss.
You could not care,
whether it is unfair.
You just do as you are pleased;
you are the boss.

Capitalism is right and communism is wrong
You got a million and he got none.
You sleep in a bed with a pillow at your head.
He sleeps on the street
with the rats at his feet,
That is capitalism,
the strong exploits the weak.

Communism is right and capitalism is wrong,
All men are equal is the chorus of the song.
Whilst privileges and corruption fuel destruction
Of that which is right,
and then all becomes wrong.

Right or wrong wrong or right,
there are always decisions to make.
Whether to marry because you got a big belly,
or whether to abort the babe.
Whether a divorcee to marry,
or whether to become a king,
Or whether to become a nun,
or from a rich man to take his ring.
Whether to be a bishop
and a father in secrecy,
Or whether to tell the world
and face the penalty.
Whether to be a married priest,
or in celibacy to stay,

And fight the sexual temptations
that haunt you night and day.
Whether to send him to prison
for a crime he did not commit,
Or whether to prosecute the police
who were the cause of it.
Whether he is a bit of a looney,
or as a murderer he should be hanged,
Whether it is your duty
that man should ever kill man
And yet you drill like mechanical robots,
marching left and right
To the programme that commands your will,
to go and kill in fight.

Yes, assholes govern nations
And in their folly they make decisions.
Their minds are twisted, their hearts corrupted,
And with blood they wash their hands.
Always they bully the weak
Never wisdom they seek.
Because their minds are twisted,
and their hearts corrupted,
And with a forked tongue they speak.
Politicians and churchmen alike
They support war as the ultimate right.
They don't have the wisdom, honour or the courage,
To settle disputes in other ways,
But only in a bloody fight.

So innocent lives they claim
And then argue over who is to blame.
It was a principle that was so valuable,
And they do the same thing again.

They'd rather you die and leave others to cry
For a cause they considered a principle.

For what's a few lives and how much are they worth?
Your principle took lives laid buried in the dirt.
Millions die and you really don't know why,
Did your principle get the lives it was worth?

That is the role of a politician
With powers up his sleeves like a magician.
He makes the rules for the people he fools,
And often at the expense of the nation.
He declares wars instead of peace
And catastrophies he unleashed.
But that is alright to have a fight,
That's what to you he preached
So you go to war not knowing what for.
He tells you it is for the good of the nation
So you killed and lamed
And you will not be blamed,
It was the duty of your station.

Men, women and children,
strangers in a different land.
People you never met,
To you they are no threat.
You showed them no mercy
You slaughtered them brutally.
Innocent people you called your enemy.

Is it right or wrong, wrong or right,
Or is it just a matter of opinion?
And the same opinion you considered wrong,
someone declared that it's right.
It is just a matter of a different view,
focused from another sight.
And it is those opinions that become the rules,
To forcefully be implemented by fools.
And they feel justified obeying their rules,
With brutality the blade of their tools.

So they beat you and rape.
What they want they just take.
And in the papers it makes good news.
Telling stories about peoples' lives,
their privacy you invade,
Just to sell to the public in black and white.
With truth and lies you defame.

You killed millions in a war,
And you are told that is within the law.
You steal from the rich to feed the poor,
But that, you are told, is against the law.
You beat up your wife and then you rape her,
Is that within or against the law?
No one cares to know; no one is sure.

Billions are spent in pursuit of war,
When right among you millions are poor.
Destructive weapons in the sky, land and sea,
A show of strength, or is it stupidity?
You would not help those who are not your race,
Their religion or politics are out of place,
And their traditional values are not of your taste.
So you leave them to starve
Although millions you have.
You prefer to see it all go to waste.

You failed in policies, one after the other,
Like disasters of unpredictable weather.
And as things got worse
With no money in your purse,
They filled you with promises that things would be better.

But man of politics, how much do you care?
Corruption and greed, brutally you lead,
And enslave the people in fear.
Your peoples' rights you abuse

With inequitable rules.
You intimidate and you persecute
And those who oppose you,
you jail or shoot.
Rights and wrongs, wrongs and rights
Your sins be with you,
damnation your plight.

You are rich and they are poor,
that is the way it will always be.
You will take all that they have and even more.
And for that you will charge a fee.
Whether it is right, or whether it is wrong
who really cares a damn?
To let them have a bit too much,
Is exactly what does the harm.

Rights and wrongs in the market place
Everyone struggling to make a living.
There is nothing that someone will never do,
for a price there is always someone willing.

Rights and wrongs in high and low places,
Among officials and prostitutes in selected palaces.
Among officials and boys in institutions
Taking advantage of situations.

Rights and wrongs are both for paupers and kings alike,
No one is above God's law.
By eternal justice you will pay for your sins,
It is the medicine that gets the soul cure.

But rights and wrongs are not just about law,
Some are the rules of the game
you must follow to score.
And without them you die,
As chaos runs wild

Like a fire consuming straw.

Consider your life and what may be
All the things you take for granted,
that made it orderly.
To play a game there must be rules,
Or how else would you win the pools?
Rights and wrongs, wrongs and rights
Shadows of the day and shadows of the night.
They are everywhere and here to stay,
They are with you every day.
They follow you around,
With you they belong.
To hell and back and under the sea
With rights and wrongs you have no privacy.

Rights and wrongs determine everything
There is a time to end and a time to begin.
A time to get up and a time to lie down,
A time to go and a time to come.
A time to eat with the people you meet.
A time to work and a time to play,
You can either go or you can stay.

You go to the moon and further beyond,
To human needs you hardly respond.
Turning right and sometimes left,
as if you don't know where to go.
And the problems you meet
On and off the street,
They are only the seeds you sow.
Is it right or is it wrong?
That is the question you want to know.
And on your journey that seems so long,
Answers are different wherever you go.

Destruction you often create

To remedy when it is too late.
You got your asshole stuck in a peg
And your head between your legs.
Your trousers in a twist
And down your legs is where you pissed.
Somebody you blame
When things are not the same,
They are getting worse
And costing you your purse.
Riots and strikes, wrongs and rights,
You had enough right up to your throat
You don't know how to vote,
For right or for wrong.

Decisions, decisions you make
Moving forward or backward, crooked or straight.
Rights and wrongs are what they are
And on your conscience they can shine or scar.
They can be measured in degrees,
some serious, some trivial,
Some rewarding and some detrimental.
And the only escape is in your burial.

You lived your life from the moment you were born,
And all things you did were either right or wrong,
You learned of their differences and their values too,
Just what you ought and ought not to do
Within your environment and all around you.

You hustle through your tunnel, drifting apart.
To keep straight on your road
you need a good start.
But who is with wisdom to guide you on,
And protect you from colliding
with that which is wrong?
Rights and wrongs, wrongs and rights,
In trials and tribulations for all your life.

Environmental Influences

Your environment is your place in this world.
It is where you live whilst growing old.
It is where you learn,
you work and you play,
It is where you do everything every day.
It is where rights and wrongs
differ from place to place,
In accordance with the culture of a different race.
It is the arena where you are trained,
To endure the daily influences bombarding your brain.
It is your home, your land, your sea and air,
And it is where your instincts are developed,
in response to what is there.
It is where you gather friends and become familiar,
With places and the many faces you do remember.
It is where you spend most of your life
Be it a hell or a paradise.

In your environment, likewise every other,
All things right and all things wrong
As they are declared in God's commandment.
They were so yesterday as they are today,
And they will continue to be so right to the end.

But rights and wrongs which are declared by man,
Are often to suit the times.
For that which was wrong yesterday becomes right today
In changes that suit mankind.

Many assholes they make the rules

Laws no better than an ass.
They spend much time,
and cannot make up their mind
And another fatuous bill simply gets passed.

You learned what is right in your environment
is that which is wrong in his.
Something with its roots deep in the mud of traditions,
And like the effects of long-taken pills.
A morbid influence upon your mind,
A cocaine with its ills.
So is your environmental influence
That to you society wills.

What are your customs that are not his
Simply because of your place of birth?
You may prefer ham and eggs
But for him it is curried goat.
And what are your values that are not his
Simply because of your place of birth?
To respect the family and their authority
Regardless of what it's worth.

You disrespect your father
and disrespect your mother,
You disrespect your sister
and disrespect your brother.
You speak your mind at will.
You lock up deep inside
Your feelings you hide.
To disrespect, emotionally kills.

The women you respect
You treat them without regret,
In a manner of inferiority.
But to you women are the same
Regardless from whence they came,

You treat them with equality.
All women you deny,
the ecstasy of the pursuing eye
To become Cinderellas in their society.
You show her love and care
Whilst you treat her grossly unfair,
With doses of psychological cruelty.

A woman, you say, she must work and be paid,
In rates the same as a man.
She must be able to vote
To wear trousers and coat,
And to do whatever she thinks she can.
But to you that is wrong
A woman is not so strong,
To shoulder the burdens of a man.
But she can work in the field
And many children she must breed,
And drink from her cup of traditions.

Environmental freedoms,
environmental restrictions,
They dictate your ways and your customs.
So you wear a suit
To look smart and cute,
And a tie that catches the eye.
But your attire, no one admires
So to catch an eye you smile.

You wear your knickers underneath
And a bra you prefer none.
You wear your bangers on your feet,
And your knickers, they are never on.
You wear rings on your fingers
That make them look attractive and pretty
You wear a ring hanging from your nose
Is it for a joke? Because it's funny

You uncover your face without disgrace,
To let your beauty be seen.
Whilst you cover up your face in every place,
Hiding from evil, it seems.

You walk the streets
with your legs exposed,
And the charms of your breast
with their secrets disclosed.
Whilst you in fine linen wrapped everything,
From the beauty of your smile
to the nails on your toes.

Your beauty and charms you reveal
And with all your sex appeal,
To fuel the flames of romantic fire.
But you keep them concealed
Both your beauty and your sex appeal,
Wrapped coldly under your attire.

You dance and embrace face to face
With warm passionate feelings.
But you will never try
And it is not that you are shy,
But that your society will never be forgiving.

You dance in the nude
and perform acts that are rude,
And your environment says that's okay
Whilst over there, no one will ever dare,
The penalty is much too heavy to pay.

You saunter in the nude
whilst you swim in the nude
Then greet each other and smile.
In an environment which is pure nature
It is the accepted behaviour

To be in your birthday suit and with pride.

In an environment of homos,
there everyone knows,
It is just the place to be.
You simply approach a lad,
he would not think that you are mad
Because he knows you want to be sexy.

Environmental influences programming your mind
Iron fist of society ensures you toe the line.
And what more did you learn
in the environment of your birth?
Woman in man's environment
she has but little hope.
She is not an equal,
that can never be.
But really it depends,
upon the common sense,
That thrives in the society.

You like to booze and gamble but lose,
And often to have a good screw.
You prefer a virgin,
so a saint you remain,
Whilst ejaculating in your hands, or in the loo.

Your women you circumsise
because you consider it wise,
To keep her pure in virginity.
And only because of your taboo laws,
Concerning sex before matrimony.

You go into the world
in a search for your girl,
But that is left for your parents to do.
You are not so bold,

you simply do as you are told.
Your parents they choose for you.

Having a dance and a song to sing,
The way it is done is the cultural thing.
The way you dress and how you move,
Your body you swing to rhythmic blues.
The way you walk and what you eat
And how you speak to the people you meet.
What you drink and how you think,
A hole in your sock and your feet stink.

Each environment with their own
Songs and dance and style of romance.
Your beliefs and imaginations of the unknown,
And your superstitions that you cannot disown.

Influences in your environments,
Support the differences in your arguments.
How you do and what you do,
Environmental traditions forced upon you.

You sit on a chair,
he sits on the floor.
It does not mean that he is poor.
But it will seem that all it means,
Is that he is from a different shore.

You carry a basket upon your head
Full of cakes and freshly baked bread.
And walk a mile to the market place,
In muddy shoes that have got no lace.
But for you, your bike will do,
You jumped on it and off you raced.

You cut the bread and he pulls at the bread,
With fingers heavy and wild.

You shake his hands; he prefers romance
So he hugs, kisses and smiles.

You say hello and in a hurry to go
You stand at your door to speak.
You say come in and have a drink
In your house is where friends do meet.

You say good day and thank you sir
And take your place in the queue.
You rush and push,
ill manners you pose
In a hurry to get to the loo.

You played at your game
and he played at his game
Each with their very own rules.
But whichever you play
they end the same way,
You either draw, win or you lose.

On camels you ride; on horse he rides.
There is no need to wonder why.
On elephants he rides; on oxes you ride.
Traditions they never die.

You wash your clothes in a river,
And sing whilst you lash them on a stone.
You wash your clothes in a machine
Right there in the kitchen of your home.

You clean with water and you dry with paper
After your visit of nature.
Both used their fingers
and this he remembers,
The way they were smelling long after.
But why the difference is it a preference,

Or just a culture passed on to son and daughter?

It is the traditions and customs
in your environment fencing you apart.
Doing things differently everywhere you went,
And in every form of art.

Consider for a moment the values you learned
Within the environment that is your home.
Traditional values plus other taboos
And every environment with their own.

You eat with silvers and you dine with sticks,
And you with your fingers dipped in the dish.
You eat snakes and you eat dogs,
You eat lizards and you eat frogs.
You eat rats and rabbits too,
But for you a nice steak will do.
You eat only fish;
you prefer vegetables,
And for you it is spaghetti and noodles.
You drink wine, and you drink vodka.
You prefer tea with your lobster;
You eat pork when you will not,
And your lamb it must be halal cut.
You like your roti but you prefer bread;
And you, everything with curry is how you are fed.
You drink milk; eat butter and cheese,
But for you it's only fresh fruits from off the trees.

But whatever you may eat,
from the land, air or sea,
Your environmental customs
decide what it should be.
In an environment accustomed to pork, beef or fish,
Whoever will dare to eat a delicious looking dish
Made up of vegetables, rat and chips,

Or cockroaches and rice flavoured with spice?
You will not try it,
no matter how nice it looks,
And no matter that it was prepared
by the very best cooks.
In your environment it is not a habit,
So your psychological response is to be sick.

Developing a taste and common sense
In response to the things in your environment,
You adapt and acquire responses to your desire
By the persuasions of the values of your traditions.

Environment of birth,
down the tunnel of his throat,
What else unto him you unleashed?
Some unpleasant accent that is never absent,
But daily with him to haunt his speech.
Environmental curse, why did you disclose
such an awesome burden to bear?
It will not leave him alone wherever he roams,
In such an awful accent to swear.
Your speech is never right,
you cannot speak in a manner polite,
And nothing that you say is clear.

You go to a doctor when you are sick
To get some tablets, or a needle prick.
But you prefer dried herbs and garlic,
With the beating of drums, wild dances and songs,
And some dried bones from a grave to do the trick.

You wrap up your head and don't cut your beard,
For reasons you don't know why.
But only because of some religious laws.
Traditional values must apply.

You pray every day and yet foolish you stay,
As an asshole to the folly of your ways.
Your traditional values are no excuse
For the manner in which you behave.

You are a Muslim and you are a Jew,
You a Christian and you a Hindu.
Your parents are the ones who decided for you,
The faith in which you communicate with the same God.
It is your environmental traditions
That are the cause of the difference,
And the conflicts of dogma among you all.

You wash yourself in a river,
In the gushing and the tumbling of dirty water.
And then you say that your sins have been washed away.
You go to the confessional
And there someone your sins you tell.
And then you say that your sins are forgiven as from today.
And then again, you go back and do the same,
More sins to wash off or to confess another day.

You pray to statues to heal your ill
And call upon your gods to heed your will.
You celebrate carnivals and different festivals
In a frenzy of exuberant thrills.
Traditional values with sacrificial taboos,
Always it's something for you to kill.

You invoke the dead and talk to spirits,
In an environment of voodoo and sorcery tricks.
You are so scared, you are afraid of the dead.
Pins are what they stuck right through your lips.

They say you are a witch and you a faith healer,
You a satanist and you a witch doctor.
You throw a coin in to a river.

Every thirteenth day in October.
You drink blood and eat raw liver,
To break the spell of the witch doctor.
You in the nude, you behave very lewd,
Satanic tricks are sexually crude.

You paint your face for wild songs and dance,
In an effort to awake the sleeping serpent.
In an ecstasy you stripped off your clothes,
As a provocative temptress is how you pose.
At the moment of eclipse to make your wish,
Nothing less for you than to get rich.

You smoke weed because you feel you must,
Hay! Everyone does it, so what's the fuss?
Under a ladder you would not walk,
And over a grave you would not talk.
Just lay the flowers which you have brought,
And slowly walk backwards away.

You bath on Fridays in magic solutions,
To rid the evil spirits from your emotions.
When in an environment of superstitions,
Skulls and crossbones and black magicians.
You become superstitious and full of fear,
Afraid of things that are not even there.
And from evil spirits to cleanse yourself,
You may be engaged in something else.
You lashed yourself heavy blows,
With an iron chain, you suffer pain,
The agony self-imposed.
And only because it is the tradition,
Which has become an environmental custom.
Superstitious beliefs of the past,
In your mind implanted forever to last.

In an environment with historical mysteries,

The things you fear are absurdities.
Opinions and views, the views and opinions,
Alive in your environment they are a forceful influence.
They determine a way of life,
Whether they are unnecessary or they are worthwhile.
You follow in the ways things are done,
So you are influenced under the sun.

You are obstinate in your belief in the old ways,
By traditional values you become enslaved.
Never to think logically
or to act and behave rationally.
It's always the old way day after day,
A step towards change is to step astray.

You fight with a bull to entertain,
And in a war-like dance you do the same.
In your masquerade body of carnival colours,
You prance up and down and sometimes for hours.

You charm snakes or cast out devils,
To be buried in the sand, in the mud or pebbles.
For all these things and whatever you do,
Your environmental influences
are preying upon you.

In your environment society is free,
So you pissed down your trousers,
and even pissed on me.
You steal my purse and sometimes do worse,
And then you go free in a democracy.

In your environment your freedom is free
That you can even practice bigamy,
With forty-one children and eleven wives,
All daughters – no sons – so still he tries.

In an environment of a dictatorship
All opinions and views are for censorship.
You cannot speak your mind
You must simply toe the line,
Or you end up in a jail ever so quick.

Friends among you cannot be trusted,
A slip of your tongue
and you could be arrested.
Or someone in your family simply disappeared,
With no explanations.
You are told that he is dead.

In an environment of a monarchy,
It is a dictatorship by a family.
They grab control of everything
To the people they leave absolutely nothing.
It is like they own the entire country
They have bank accounts swollen with money.
They control with spies
everywhere like flies,
Just one word of criticism
and you will be sorry.

Every environment has its own politics,
Many who rule are assholes and hypocrites.
Some are benevolent, some ruthless,
Some try to do their best.
Some are feeble-minded, corrupt and selfish,
They use their office for their own interest.
Some are deceiving and conniving,
They will tell you almost anything.
There are a few who are really sincere,
For the welfare of their people, they really care.
They work hard and for them it ends sad,
Swiftly they are removed from their chair.

An environment constructed in graceful beauty
And an environment distastefully ugly.
In one there is wealth,
in the other poverty.
Both have values of their own,
And traditional cultures with seeds well sown.

Environment of poverty, birth place of illiteracy,
Homeland of vagrancy.
In squalor and filth you sleep,
What you did not sow you reap.
Your life is really hell
When you are not doing well,
Feelings of despair run deep.

The environment of poverty
is a gutter place unhealthy.
And when in the gutter you make your bed,
The sewage of society gathers moss in your head.
And clouds your thoughts of common sense.
So you think as a fool and act as a mule,
And often at someone else's expense.

You cannot smell, touch, hear nor see,
How much the gutter influences your mentality.
To advice you seldom listen,
And do foolish things without good reason.
That if by some good stroke of luck,
You manage to escape from the filth and rot.
The gutter mentality you take with you,
And continue to be an asshole in whatever you do.

In the environment of poverty, filth and squalor,
There hygiene standards are low.
There's where you learn the things of the gutter,
And there that is what you will always know.

In an environment full of crime,
Lives are in danger all the time.
You feel the chill of a haunting fear
Though you tried to pretend it is never there.
Corruption thrives as honesty dies,
The name of the game is to survive.

Pickpocketing, rapes, theft,
assaults, prostitution and vice,
The law is an ass on which the criminal rides.
Dog eats dog and cat eats cat,
Nothing much is left for the rat.

Environment of crime like the environment of prayer,
The link which is common is the existence of fear.
Fear of the known, the unknown, something or the other,
It is either your life or your soul in danger.

In an environment of beauty and envious wealth,
Life is comfortable, even when you are in bad health.
And the influences that grab hold of your mind,
Although they may be hostile as well as kind.
They are the forces of literacy,
That inspire you into thinking positively.
And you grow up developing your mind,
When in such an environment
you are bound to do fine.

An environment of love
an environment of hate,
Attitudes developed are intensely great.
The things you hear, smell, see and feel,
To your senses they may appeal.
And what you love and what you hate,
From the seeds of your environment they dissipate.

City environment and country environment,

Both with cool breeze blowing in the air.
One with peace and serenity,
The other with a noise that drums at your ear.
One so clean and fresh,
It soothes the pain in your chest.

The other so foul and contaminated,
With its destruction grossly underated.
One with the influences of the spoils
That heats your burning desire until it boils.
With doors wide open to temptations.
You cannot ignore the provocations.
The other with influences ever so gentle
It is almost like living in a holy temple.
There things are so peaceful,
The people so graceful.
Not a sound to be heard
but the whistling of a bird,
And life goes on ever so simple.

Traditional values and customs
That are the cultures of different nations.
Here I mention just a few
Of the influences daily pressuring you.
Programming you towards your society's needs,
And each environment with their very own,
Rooted from the seeds that have been sown.
And it is the one in which you are raised,
That determines the culture of your ways.
Your environment is where it is decided for you,
The status quo for your whole life through.

Law and Order

It was a big bang,
The uncanny moment before time began.
The mighty explosion of explosions,
And from which all other explosions exploded.
And then it settled with shape and form,
In distances forgotten,
and where time did never dawn.

Into an endless and boundless omneity
Where things were either born,
or they appeared mysteriously.
Well, that is what science has said,
And that it happened over millions of years.
A powerful explosion,
Followed by a chain of fusions,
Which brought into being masses of substance
Never to be grasped by your comprehension.

And from all the eruptions caused,
After the turmoil of universal star wars.
Appeared most victoriously
Was the birth of an infinity,
With powers of destruction and tranquillity,
And with the name universe.

And within it your world was born
With size and shape and with form,
From the numerous particles exploded.
It claimed its place in the universe
And suckled creatures blessed and cursed.

And with powers to eliminate
Those it could no longer tolerate.

Yes, a big bang may have led
To the formation of a heaven and a hell.
Stars and Mars, sun and moon,
And the billions of other things
that appeared, either late or soon.

But how do you explain
Just what governs those things?
The laws that they strictly obey,
In every galactic way.
Did the laws emerge from the big bang too,
And without mass and velocity?
How very certain could that be,
Perhaps a miracle, magic or a mystery.

In this endless far-reaching universe,
Where science has boldly encroached,
Discovering only more and more
the existence of nature's rules
Which no bang could have possibly produced.
For it is something or someone greater than that,
And if asked to be exact,
Then you can proclaim
On the authority of your name,
That it can only be a God.

Just you tarry for a while
And look up into the sky.
Now look all around you
Upon things old and upon things new.
Take a close look at nature
And observe carefully its sophisticated behaviour.
Now what do you see,
Are things in disorder

or are they orderly?

All around you is a display of order
And where there is order, there must be rules.
And when you have rules,
There must be a creator of the rules.
Rules cannot just appear
From out of nowhere.
Rules are neither subjects nor objects,
They have no mass
Nor movement slow or fast.

Bangs and explosions may harness chains of fusion.
But never can a bang nor an explosion,
Whether it be small, medium or grand,
In space, air, sea or land,
Explode and create a phenomenon of rules.
No gasses can form,
Or from an orgasm be born, a law or a rule.

And that is because law is an abstract,
It is without lean and without fat.
It has no energy and it has no weight,
It cannot be taken or be put on a plate.
It is simply and only the rule.

Rules in the galaxies of the universe exist,
And in your world, in science and mathematics.
And even in the lines of a poetic verse,
And in the duties of the kind and caring nurse.

Science cannot disprove that there is law in nature,
Neither can science disprove that there is natural order.
But science cannot yet calculate who is the creator,
Neither can he, in his laboratory, discover the maker
Of the inscrutable laws of nature.

You make machines applying scientific rules
Which are the same in every language and in every school.
You never divide when you should square,
Or you will never find the answer there.
Nor do you subtract when you should add,
Or the result could be very sad.
And whenever you are in search for a technical answer,
You must always apply the correct formula.
Any mistakes in applying the rule,
Could result in you been taken for a fool.

You can observe that in nature laws are obeyed,
And even in the heavens where peace prevailed.
And in a boundless universe of law and order,
Without the rules it can only be disaster.

Laws of gravity and relativity,
Laws of chance and romance and of probability.
Laws of electro magnetism and thermodynamics,
Laws of electrostatics and quantum physics.

All these laws are no accidental mystery
That came about from explosions deep under the sea.
Or from a bang big or small,
That eventually developed into laws.
Neither were they made by man
In a factory, or the frying pan.
But they could have appeared from his laboratory,
Not as an invention, but a discovery.
And without these laws that nature obeys,
Without them, how will things behave?

Disasters in space as objects race across the universe
from galaxy to galaxy.
With catastrophies from here to there,
A universal star wars declare,
The wrath of destruction everywhere.

How tall should trees grow,
what fruits should they bear?
Where on your face should your nose appear?
Why doesn't any tree reach up to the sky?
What tells it to stop when it reaches so high?
Why doesn't the snake grow legs and run?
Is it because crawling on its belly is a lot more fun?
You carry your balls hanging between your legs,
Why not around your neck,
or at the back of your ears?
Lions eat meat, elephants eat leaves,
Horses race on land, monkeys swing on trees.
Fishes in the sea, birds in the air,
Man on land, How they all got there?

And amidst the dangers in the wild,
Creatures live and die.
Taking care of their kind among their own species,
They live as families with responsibilities.
In the natural order of things they survive.
And who decides all these things,
their shape and their size
Where should be their tail,
and where should be their eyes?
Are they not all governed by the rule,
the natural laws they obey
Written into their genes from creation day?

That is the order of life and how things are,
Instructed by their genes, nature's messenger.
It is only with law that order can exist,
Take it away and the wind blows chaotic.

Laws in the sky, in the heavens and in hell,
Laws in the entire universe as well.
Laws in your world and in your environment,
Laws in your home and everywhere you went.

Laws in science, you must apply the rule,
To calculate the risk, or you die as a fool.
Mathematical laws in formulae expressed,
Wrongly applied could have disastrous effects.

Laws in the playing field
and in the boxing ring,
To play a game of cards, table tennis or anything.
Consider trying to play a game
when you don't know the rules.
Then how do you play;
how do you decide who win or who lose?

It is the rules that perfect the game?
Without the rules, it will not be the same.
With rules in sports recognised internationally,
Worldwide the same games can be played properly.
And in competitions of any kind
and wherever they are,
And among you with different cultures
that which doesn't matter.
The one thing that is common among all those who enter,
By the same rules of the game
you play with one another.

And in your language as it is in sport,
There are the rules which you are taught.
Rules in your language enable you to speak,
Fluently with the people you meet.
And to communicate in writing properly,
To transmit your messages sensibly.
It could not have been done without the rules,
Which you learned about your language in your schools.

And as in language, in music too
There are the rules which exist for you.
It is the rules in music

Which direct you to compose it
In the manner in which you do.

Laws international and laws institutional,
Religious laws to aid the spiritual.
Laws in superstitions and taboo,
Through your fears and ignorance
are the asshole things you do.

Matrimonial laws and company laws,
Aviation laws and navigation laws.
Criminal laws and property laws,
Traffic laws, environmental laws,
bye laws and idiotic laws.
Laws in and out of wars.

A law for this and a law for that,
A law for almost everything.
And where there is no law,
There is where disorder steps in.

There are many rules that restrict your life,
Even in the freedoms of democracy.
You cannot steal or murder,
but you can beat your wife,
A common practice in society.
You cannot light a fire just to damage property,
That would be malicious and unfriendly.
You can speak your mind
and say things unkind,
But that depends upon your society.
You can do this, but you cannot do that,
They are numerous and many
And without them which are the rules,
Society would be a catastrophe.

Rules to determine your behaviour,

Whether it is good or bad manners, or whatever.
Whether it is acceptable what you have done,
From many the rules you cannot run.

The daily order of things you take for granted,
Your comings and your goings however they are restricted.
They are influenced by laws,
the hard and easy rules implemented.
To maintain order in your environment,
The aim of the objective is crimes to prevent.
And they can be achieved successfully,
By the enforcement of discipline within society.

Having rules and laws without proper enforcement,
Is like the issuing of a cheque without an endorsement.
When rules are made they must be enforced,
Or their principal purpose is completely lost.

Your miserable life you claimed was successful,
Without the rule of law,
it could have been most regretful.
You could have been raped many times over,
With no one to turn to, no law, no order.
You could have been robbed of all your wealth.
Then what would you have done?
Thank God for your health.

Could you for a moment imagine what may be?
Use your mind's eye and try to see,
Without the rule of law the catastrophe,
The disorders and disasters and the pornography.
The drugs, AIDS, rapes and murders,
The assaults and larcenies and the joyriders.
And what would you do
when there's no law to turn to?
No redress; society is in a mess.

No church or homes or schools and hospitals.
Survival is for the fittest of the criminals.
Nothing that you take for granted will ever be,
Without the rule of law,
nothing could be orderly.

You may be intelligent and even be wise,
But without law there's no paradise.
Rules, laws and discipline,
Whenever enforced justice must reign.
When rules are broken or even bent,
Disorders are hastened to a regrettable end.

Justice is to the law,
as the law is to punishment,
Crimes committed are often by instrument.
Some are premeditated, some accidental,
Some are driven by hate,
and some by the psycho mental.
Some for lust and some for greed,
Some from an impulse or a compelling need.
Some for absolutely no cause whatsoever,
You just can't stand the damn nigger.
Some for spite, for love, or just for fun,
But for whatever the reason,
let justice be done.

For when ever justice cries, injustice rides high,
And with full speed ahead.
And thereupon disorder strides,
Upon the grounds where the law is dead.
But how do you construct a puzzle,
When the pieces do not fit?
How is justice to be done,
When the punishment for the crime hardly matches it.

When laws are made by fools and assholes,

Criminals escape through a net of loopholes.
And not until those holes are plugged,
Justice is nothing but an Irish mug.
And how can justice be really just
When the law itself is unjust?
A ludicrous decision decisively passed,
To become the law, or is it an ass?
Justice or injustice,
only one can be done
And it is for you to decide,
which will be the one.

Fear and Beliefs

I shall begin by quoting
The well known biblical phrase,
"man know thyself".

Without a choice into this world you came,
And perhaps most likely in vain.
But only for a brief moment of time,
And then to return from whence you came,
And perhaps, who knows? You may come back again,
Through the unwitting years in your life
The period of your incomprehensions.

And during those years of your unblemished innocence,
Your only years untouched by fears and beliefs
That many dangers you dared,
and to your parents' grief.
And that was only because,
You were without beliefs and doubts.
You had not yet developed your instincts,
You were without learning
and without understanding.
And most of all, you were totally void
Of the prevalence of fear.

You would have boldly confronted a lion,
A deadly serpent or a dragon.
In fact, any danger or disaster of any kind.
And without a tremble or a shiver,
A sound of fear, or nervousness, or whatever.
A galvanised heartbeat

Or a terrified sweat upon your cheek.

You would have crawled from a window high up in the sky
Just to land on a cloud to steal a ride
And only because the cloud was there.
And upon the ocean waters to walk
you would have tried
Boldly and daringly and with a smile.

But as your mind developed,
With your senses and instincts whilst growing up
You consciously became aware
Of the things that caused you pain,
both slight and severe.
Some you were able to endure,
But most you could not bear.

You became acquainted
to your drumming heart's impulses,
And to the trembles, the sweat and the nervousness,
To the stiffness and the numbness
And to the invisible, the intolerable and unbearable
Frequent and unwelcome visits by fear.

And so you developed,
more rapidly than growing up,
An awareness of fear of the things that threatened you with
    pain.
The impetuous fire dangerously threatening.
The natural disasters: an earthquake,
Heavy winds, rain and thunder
The hurricane in a stormy weather.
The muddy wild waters gushing down the river,
And beating upon boulders with tremendous power.

The revengeful wounded tiger,
The savage dog that bites,

Bridges with their terrifying heights.
A poisonous snake in the grass,
The deadly spider creeping up your arse.
The hungry lions in the wild,
The mad dog with rabies or irritating piles.
The dreaded bees high up in the trees,
The lethal gasses in the air,
drifting with the breeze from here to there.
The hangman's rope,
A blade at your throat.
The sharks in the sea,
the crocodiles in the river,
A nagging mother, your drunken father.
Your jealous sister, an irate brother,
The bully in your school, and the unruly thugs.
The thief in your house, a murderer and rapist,
The corrupted politician
and the irascible dentist.
The police and the jailer,
The inquisitive and malicious neighbour.

You are afraid even to tell the truth
and afraid to tell a lie,
Because someone has threatened you
and you are afraid to die.
But you are afraid only when you are threatened,
at some time or the other,
Of that moment that may appear,
with pain for you to suffer.
You fear that moment that may suddenly come
to visit upon you pain
In an envelope full of dangers,
that may leave you dead or lame.
But when that threat has vanished and gone,
You become yourself again.

So it is clear that it is pain you fear

And not the things that are before you there.
You fear not a butterfly,
Nor the rainbow high up in the sky.
You fear not the dogs that bark,
as long as they do not bite.
You fear not the great white shark,
as long as it stays out of sight.
You fear not those who are gentle and kind,
Or the dazzling sun that shines.
Nor the peaceful breeze that blows
From east to west or wherever it goes.
You fear not the gentle rain,
As long as with it,
it brings you no pain.

But you are afraid of the tiger in the wild,
It may grip at your throat,
and in pain you'll die.
So this you know, that it is pain you have feared,
And all its messengers,
of them you are scared.
Everything that can cause you some form of pain,
And from your eyes bring tears that drop like rain.

You fear the things also that emotionally hurt,
That increase your heartbeats,
or swell the lump in your throat.
You are afraid to be with the one you love
for reasons of your own,
Afraid to be seen with her or with him;
gossips will not leave you alone.

Afraid of your sex, it makes you vexed
Wondering if you did screw her well,
Or would she prefer to have another go
With someone else in bed.
You don't want to lose her and that you know,

To work far away from home you will never go.
You are afraid to trust and to distrust,
In matters of sex, your compulsive lust.

You fear things which you cannot see,
And can neither smell nor touch
or predict will be.
Fear of the unknown, the uncertainty.
If your belly will swell,
And your soul lost in hell
Because of your sex before matrimony.

Fear of the battle that you may lose,
Your wife, your job –
there are times you must choose.
Your exam results after studying so hard,
Did you make the grade?
You are afraid it's bad.

Afraid of your weaknesses and the wine you sip
The women you laid, they could make you sick.
The many lovers in and out of your bed,
Are they with AIDS?
But how could you tell?

Afraid that your husband will never come back,
Each time he steps out and heads for the track.
Afraid of the booze and the money he may lose,
But afraid most of all that he may get the sack.

You made a bet and now you are afraid to lose your money.
It may cause you regret
should your children go hungry.
And then what will you do?
You really do not know.
To show your face at home,
you are afraid to go.

Afraid to hurt the ones you dearly love,
And yet you punched them with your tongue,
not wearing gloves.
Delivering blows to their head and their heart,
With your painful words you smashed them apart.
And then you are afraid of what you have done,
It was not right, so it's got to be wrong.

You are so much afraid that he may die,
A bullet was shot right through his eye.
You are worried, uneasy and terrified,
To be left as a widow and with a child.
You are afraid of what may be,
A future full of uncertainty
And daunted perhaps by misery.

Afraid that you may be left forgotten hanging on the shelf,
A housewife you want to be and nothing else.
You are so pretty and full of vigour,
Sadly you cannot find the right feller.
You are so cautious you pick and choose,
The good ones who come along you swiftly lose.

Afraid that all your chances are running out,
You are getting older and without a doubt
Afraid of the opportunities all passing you by,
And not one could you grab,
and you do not know why.

You are afraid of the audition you may fail,
You are nervous and shaking
like a puppy dog's tail.
You are sweating all over
You cannot pull yourself together.
You look like a person who's being taken to jail.

Fear of love and fear of hate

The troubles they cause are often too great.
And during those moments you don't know who to trust,
You do foolish things that you feel you must.

However naïve or unjust,
You do them willingly or unwillingly just the same.
It is never yourself, but someone else to blame.
Doing wrong things, and yet afraid of the consequences.
Someone else always to pay for your offences.

Afraid of the erupting market forces
That damage and destroy many businesses.
Afraid of the daily rising prices,
You cannot get to the roots of the causes.
And to secure a grip on inflation,
And the dispersing thick fog
from the clouds of recession.

Afraid now of losing your empire,
The good life, the influence and the power.
With both friends and conmen all mixed together,
You certainly will need a Sherlock Holmes' detector.

Afraid of the politician and his policy,
Of stringent measures to strengthen the economy.
With unemployment rising high,
And discontent darkening the sky.
No more rises in your salary,
You are left to struggle with difficulty.

Afraid of the shark in the waters of bankruptcy,
It could rip you to pieces whenever it chooses,
And destroy you financially.
And affect the lifestyle of your family,
With the loss of your friends,
your neighbours and the good company
That you were accustomed to.

Afraid that you wouldn't know what to do
And that you may perpetrate suicide,
You want to live and you are afraid to die.
And when you think seriously about it,
You are attacked by fear with a riveting grip.
So you decide that in death you won't hide,
But you will stay alive and face the music.

And live with or without your fears whilst growing old,
Even of death, as it draws near to claim your soul.
The changes in your body, your senile mentality,
You are afraid that you are losing your sexual sensitivity.
And the power of your erection,
With its stiffness in expansion.
You are afraid that should it all be lost.
Someone else may supply her with the erotic force.

You are afraid of disasters and instability,
And the political disorders in your society.
You fear the reprisals that you may cause,
In your fight against unjust laws.
And your case before the jury you may not win.
You are afraid you may be sent to prison for someone else's
   sin.
Murders, thefts, larceny and rapes in a riot town,
You are afraid that your house may be burnt down.
You are afraid to disobey your order,
So innocent people you mercilessly slaughter.
In the madness of war,
the game your nation plays.
You are afraid to refuse
Because your life you may lose.
You are not as brave and courageous as they say.

You just follow the crowd
like a maddened bunch of dogs,
Programmed to kill

in the name of a falsely justified cause.
So you slaughter and you butcher,
And without even thinking things over.
And only because to disobey your orders you're afraid
That you will be court marshalled and thrown into gaol
So to save your ass,
you killed, killed and killed.

You are afraid of the truth
and what it will reveal,
So you insist on the lies
you want to believe.
You plunder and you threaten,
you beg and appeal.
With your lies you are ready to make a deal.

Afraid that your friend may betray your trust,
For thirty pieces of silver,
he may feel he must.
Or in torture he may just
Be too scared and afraid.
Afraid that the rescue you need may never come.
When you cannot swim in deep water
you can only drown.
When you are innocent,
it is better not to run.

Afraid that you may never walk again,
It is no one's fault
you have just yourself to blame.
You stole a car and raced
as if it was just a game.
It is the price you must pay
now that you are lame.

Afraid of the truth and only you know why,
No one must know, wherever you go,

You would prefer to die.
Afraid that someone will find out
and bring disgrace upon you,
The brutal rape and murder that you committed
and thought that no one knew.
Afraid of yourself,
your conscience and nightmares,
The mental tortures that seem to be
lasting for years.
Afraid of the things
that may visit upon you shame,
And deep into the mud,
there to bury your name.
But there is no escape
and nowhere to run,
Neither from yourself
nor the wicked things that you have done.

You are afraid also
of the decisions you have to make,
Are they right or are they wrong?
The answer lies in faith.
You are a homo, and you are afraid
that your friends will get to know,
Because they say that it is degrading.
You are afraid of yourself,
You cannot think of anything else,
Deep inside is where you are hurting.

Afraid of so many painful things in your life,
The piranha in the water
and the attacker with a knife.
The cancer in your breast,
The pain on your chest.
You are even afraid
that you haven't done your best.

Fear of the things that are never in sight,
Like the shadows in the darkness of a stormy night.
Fear of the rain drops,
some heavy, some light,
Dripping from your rooftop
just to bring you fright.

The sound of the owl
and the fox that howls,
The whistling breeze,
the horse that sneezed.
Every quiet and every sound
Your own heartbeats
that pound like a drum.

Fear of the ghost that vanishes into the air,
Now it is gone and now it is here.
And of spirits of the dead
that are not even there
They got you so scared,
frozen stiff on your chair.

Fear of the stories that your mum and dad tell,
How the devil will chain you
and beat you up in hell.
How witches are burnt and bitches raped,
And are left to die on a cross or on a stake.
Your tongue will be pulled out
and your eyes will swell,
You will be hanged upside down
and left to swing like a bell.

Fear of the vampire that haunts at night,
And the werewolf that accidentally caught your sight.
You locked up your doors extremely tight,
You would not even switch off the light.
And you go to sleep with a cross,

attached to your right.

And with your imagination running wild
causing tremors in you deep down inside.
Then a peaceful sleep you are denied.
Because you are too much afraid.

Afraid of the stairs that lead to nowhere,
And creaks during the night,
just for you to hear.
Is it pain or is it death
that is waiting out there,
Or a treacherous demon to befriend your soul?
To lead you into hell is its only goal.

Afraid of the grave that may swallow you whole,
Or in the universe to roam as a restless soul.
The present and the thereafter,
You are even afraid to live forever.

You believed in a God high above,
And a devil in a hellhole whom no one loves.
You believed in gods everywhere,
Everything must be taken in good care.
A god of love and a god of hate,
A god of wealth and a god of health.
A god of the sun and a god of the moon,
A god of curses and good fortune.
A god of good harvest and the rain,
A god for when things go wrong, for you to blame.

You believed in curses from the gods you have offended,
Instead of the reality of natural causes.
A pain in your neck,
in your arse or in your stomach,
It is just an evil spirit causing havoc.
You are possessed, maybe, by the spirit djinn,

And to be rid of it you must be condemned to beatings.

You believed in the incarnation,
The resurrection and damnation
And in the superstitions of your long-held traditions.
Eternal life after death
and the life before, is just a preparation,
Your thoughts are entangled in a web of confusion.

You just do not know what to believe,
In your world of superstitions,
you are easily deceived.
You are afraid of the predictions written in your stars,
On Friday the thirteenth you never drive cars.
And when a bird shits upon your head,
That is very lucky,
you will never be hungry,
You will always be fed.

Some things you believed in when you were a child,
You become an adult
and those beliefs you hide.
Others are senseless and hardly worthwhile,
You bury those in you until you die.
Some beliefs you put away
To be used on the occasional day.
For a feast or a ceremony,
and in the traditional way
Passed down through generations
and in your culture to stay.

But you do not believe in superstitious things,
You are so very clever,
you know what the future brings.
No place for you to go
to suffer for your sins,
You simply rot in your grave

until nothing remains.

But many of you with your doubts and beliefs,
Your reasons are often senseless, to say the least.
Many of the things you believed
are the very things you fear,
An opium rooted in traditions
from the seeds of a superstitious scare.
But what does it matter
when a normal life you lead?
As long as your beliefs and fears are not intruders
That cause your heart to bleed.

And now that you understand
what your fears are all about,
And what is to believe
and what is to doubt.
Most of your fears are of the things that you know,
The realities in life,
the way things go.
The rest of your fears are of uncertainties
Some are superstitious and the others
just the things you believe.

It is an impulse switched in your mind,
Inherited in your nature that is not too kind.
But you can control it before it spells disaster,
It can be measured in degrees, or somehow or the other.
Small fears, great fears can buckle up your knees,
They can give you a shock, or make you freeze,
Afraid to move but carefully and with ease.

Fear makes you tremble and sometimes sweat,
Or you get so nervous
that you lost your breath.
It weakens you as it uses up your energy,
To pump up your heart in motion vigorously.

You live your life in and out of fear,
And often, you are given a warning
when it will appear.
And whenever it comes it hunts you down,
Especially when it remains with you for very long.
You don't want to eat
and you cannot even sleep,
And all you can hear
are your own heartbeats.

Fear is a friend that is not so friendly,
And that's why it is often mistaken for an enemy.
But whenever it's with you
either as a friend or a foe,
Fear is something which,
it's better you didn't know.

But belief is something totally different,
Although, like fear,
you took it with you wherever you went.
Beliefs are about things you do not know,
So you choose to believe that they are really so.
When you know, there is no need to believe,
And because you know,
you cannot be deceived.

Truth and Lies

Truth and lies, well,
what do you know about truth and lies?
Truth lives forever,
lies eventually die.
Truth existed from the beginning of time,
In a universe of splendours, mysteries and beauty.
It was created at the time of the big bang,
To record all incidents as its endless duty.

Taking notice of everything,
Doing its job day out and day in,
Recording events in the wind.
In every corner of the universe,
Whatever happened truth made note.
Nothing escaped unrecorded
From the moment truth was created.

Truth did its job without competition,
Without interference, mistakes or deception.
Truth was alone; a competitor was never known.
Until that day when you appeared
After so many millions of years.
And you created a dangerous competitor.
From your mouth out came the deceitful stranger
Whom you introduced as a partner
Alongside truth to reign forever.

A damning brute with a cursed name, 'Lie'
Which, just to mention, can cause you pain.
And an impious task you assigned to it,

To destroy truth, and to do it quick.

And never again were things the same,
Many disasters lies had claimed.
Among friends and families,
institutions and societies,
Lies arrived, to the rescue of their needs.
And always at someone's expense,
Lies crippled truth's feeble defence.

Truth had to fight to be heard,
Receiving cruel and damaging blows.
Truth had been hammered and badly twisted,
And more than often it was made distorted.
It was brutally pushed aside,
Only to make room for a lie.
It was ignored because it made you bored,
It has been despised and substituted for lies.
Your entire world of truth,
at a flick it darkens,
When a lie takes a grip
and its influence tightens.

Have you ever told a lie,
And then started to cry?
Wishing that you could die,
Because of what you have done.
Realising how disastrous were the consequences.

Have you ever told a lie just to save yourself
You passed the blame on to someone else.
And only because you were a coward,
To face the music you couldn't be bothered.

The truth as well as lies,
they both can hurt,
They can cause disasters

and that's no joke.
You can go to prison or lose a friend,
And then all things good come to an end.
But when lies hurt the pain is more severe,
To be wrongfully punished is a price too dear.

Truth can be vicious as well as kind,
It is registered in the wind and upon your mind.
It is written upon the walls all around you,
That very moment, each and everything you do.
It is also written in the history books,
And painted into pictures,
then hung by hooks.
Engraved in stones and planted upon graves,
Taught in schools and told as fairy tales.
And at unexpected moments
it can bring you worry,
It was your son who was hit
by a runaway lorry.

Truth is about you,
It is about anything and everything,
when, where and what you do.
It is what you said,
What you did in and out of bed.
What you eat and what you wear,
And what you did in the toilet
whilst you were there.
It is about how you look,
your face and your hair.
What you gave and what you take
Whether you do or do not care.

It is about that which you saw,
Whether it was within or against the law.
And yet truth is so often denied
Its rightful place in justice's eye.

Truth is often humble, simple and plain,
Lie is more convincing
when in a make-up that looks the same.
Unfortunately so often,
lies are mistaken for truth.
But then, how do you decide
What is truth and what are lies?
When lies can look as good as truth,
Dressed in disguise, looking smart and cute.
Lies can even look sexy,
Fooling men, women, everybody.
Lies can pose as a man, or a woman,
And look much better than truth ever can.

Then how one from the other could you recognise?
Unless you know the truth,
only then can you know lies.
Truth is often discarded
and lies regarded to detrimental ends.
And both whenever they hurt,
sometimes you lose your very good friends.

Truth is frequently rejected,
And sometimes never wanted.
And when by a child it is presented,
no one wants to know.
The child you accused of stealing,
When the only thing he stole was the show.
The quiet little boy who saw a murder,
The father who sexually assaulted his daughter,
But she is just a youth.
From her no one will accept the truth.
A husband who battered his wife,
A princess who took her own life,
The doctor who assaulted his patient,
The policeman who lost his patience.
The king who is a bastard,

And the president who is a homosexual.
The priest, to say the least, he is a womaniser.
The woman with whom he eloped,
She is the wife of the prime minister.

All those are truths you do not want to hear,
Although they are hammering loud at your ear.
Your husband, your wife who had an affair.
But the truth, you prefer to bury it,
Lest it be a recipe for malicious gossip.
So you hide the truth,
it must not come out,
Someone you paid to shut his mouth.
Or sometimes you even kill
To make certain that the truth will never be spilt.

Those are the times when you welcome lies,
To hide your crimes and the tears from your eyes.
So with a lie you find someone to frame,
To be wrongfully accused
and disgraced be his name.
Lies are often a disappointing friend,
Whenever you choose to put your trust in them.
Lies like snakes they have no legs,
Yet swiftly move without bruising their heads.

Take, for example, some products advertised,
They tell you about them so many lies.
This washing powder washes whiter than snow,
So why don't you buy it and have a go?
You want to get rich, I know how,
Send for the booklet with your money right now.
You will never be bald,
you will grow slim and tall,
Your face will always look young,
And your muscles become strong.
No more pimples and no more wrinkles,

And upon your breasts some sweet looking nipples.
Your skin will be smoothe, soft and nice,
And if you use this product you will always be wise.
And before going to bed, take a bit of that,
It is the only way to reduce your fat.
And although you may have a craving appetite,
It will not be for food
But for sex right through the night.
Take this daily it will make you bright,
And don't you worry,
just send me your money,
Whatever your problems
they will be put right.

When lies are even just a little disguised,
To tell the truth from lies you need to be wise.
Courts have been fooled by purgery,
And persuasive lies convinced the jury.
Learned men in high offices,
Recognised with titles as magistrates and judges.
The truth they quite often reject with disdain,
And a punishment of imprisonment
upon the innocent, they proclaim.

Kings have fallen and some lost their head.
Peasants have been hanged
and robbed of their land,
Some were jailed and brutally flogged,
Some to the death they were cruelly tortured.
Armies fell and millions lay dead.
Markets tumbled, economies crumbled
families destroyed.
Some lost their tongue,
a limb or their eyes,
But whatever it was,
it was due to lies.

Many of you, and conscientiously you do,
burden yourselves with pride.
You fooled everybody by pretending to be,
living a life of a lie.
You fooled the masses of the lower classes
From upon your horse grazing in high places.
Governments, politicians, institutions and churches,
They inject you with lies
in large and small doses.
They want to make a change
from one policy to the next,
So they deceitfully tell you
it is for your best.
They disseminate lie after lie,
And you like a fool, you never ask why.

Not that you will ever will get a truthful answer.
But to ask a question is always better.
Let them be troubled to explain,
For eventually you'll know that they are lying again.

Lies rooted firmly in traditions become the norm,
They have been in existence long before you were born.
The truth has simply been pushed aside,
Or sent to the grave with someone who died,
To be replaced by a parlous lie.

Lies to control and influence your life,
By someone with a tongue as sharp as a knife.
Lies about almost everything they tell you,
They tell you this and they tell you that
And something else is what they do.

They send you to war to protect some interest,
Which they say is for the good of your country.
To slaughter and to kill people you don't even know,
But they tell you that they are your enemy.

They don't really care about you and your business,
Neither do they care about your family.
As long as you work to protect their interest,
There's nothing for which you should worry.

Lies they shout promising you the world,
A big rise in pensions
for all those who are old.
No more poll tax, VAT, life and death tax,
Just you leave your wallet for the treasury's axe.

Reforms, free elections and democracy,
All political prisoners will be set free.
Freedom of the press, shops filled with the best,
And your pockets loaded with plenty of money.
Just you make sure that you voted for me.
And if you can read, then read my lips,
And tell me if they lie.
No more taxes is what I say,
No more, until I die.

But political lies are but just a few,
Compared with the superstitious lies told to you.
They are so many and all claim to be true,
Hardly any can be proven,
not even one or two.

Consider if this is a sin, or if it is not:
You be in love with your girlfriend
And you in love with your wife.
Each couple living together
a respectable, honest and a decent life.
Both were embraced in coition,
both performing the same,
Not in hate but in love
and in delight their orgasm came.
To share in joy, as they give their love.

In a mystical flow from one to the other.
They love each other very much.
You can only be jealous of a life as such.
And yet one lives in sin and not the other,
And for their love not hate,
they will burn forever
In Satan's hell of eternal fire.
Is that truth, or is it a lie?
This one you must work out before you die.

Since you created lies,
they have been unsparingly used,
By children and their parents,
teachers and presidents, and without excuse.
You told little lies and big lies,
You told black lies and white lies.
Some serious and some trivial,
Some led to someone's burial.
Some were meant to be funny, as a joke,
Aimed at a female friend or a bloke.
But they were not always funny,
And did not amuse anybody,
What you meant to be a joke it did hurt.

And from that moment of your creation of the lie
The truth has been battered and bruised.
And made the world in which you live and die
A place notoriously confused.
That whenever evidence is presented to you
It is for you to choose.
Lies from the truth, for you to decide,
In a case to win or lose.

You in your world and in your environment,
Among your friends and strangers everywhere you went.
You are noted to be very well learned and wise.
You have invented many things,

By the creative ingenuity of your brains.
You have created art, music and beauty,
You have constructed an abundance of luxury
For your comforts and for your needs.
You have intruded upon the stars,
And landed upon the moon and Mars.
You have discovered the very secrets of life,
The sex of a child is the choice of a wife.
You have ingeniously planned, organised and developed,
Your enquiring mind, it will never stop.

And yet to this day, you're still unable to decide,
What you were told that has been done,
Whether it was the truth or a lie.
This world, your only world,
you made unpleasant to live in and die,
When truth stares at you direct in the eyes,
you turn away your face,
And not because you are shy,
or to hide from shame and disgrace,
But to welcome a lie,
shake hands and embrace.
Justice will always be denied
to the human race.

But if in your world you got rid of lies,
Catch hold of them wherever they hide.
With an aim and determination to annihilate,
Death to the lie, be its only faith.
Then you will have laid the foundations for a better world,
Where everyone can be trusted,
because you can take their word.
And never again in your life
to be wrongfully accused,
To be punished, dismissed or even abused.
Or to lose your wife
and even your life,

And only because of a lie.

The path of justice would be so much easier,
No need then for a defending lawyer.
Because when the lie becomes extinct,
Then truth again can reign,
Just as it did in the beginning.

Offender and Offended

What is it to offend? a question asked.
To offend is to hurt, to do unto another
That which is to his displeasure,
In any way or the other.

And how do you offend? A question asked:
You offend when with your word or your deed.
You inflict upon another,
some discomfort to feel.
And for everyone offended
there is an offender,
Motivated by his reasons, but,
sometimes with none whatsoever.

Now think for a moment and try to remember,
The many times you have been offended,
And the many times you have offended.
And how many times it was meant as a joke,
And how many times it was meant to hurt?

As the night follows day
and day follows night,
You have been offended and you have offended
Sometimes very seriously
and sometimes just slight.
You offended someone or the other,
Just to satisfy your urge or desire,
Or your impulse for a little pleasure
at someone's expense.

You offended sometimes simply as a joke,
In a search of a laugh to share with a bloke.
And then only to find
that your joke was not kind.
So an offence was returned to you with an intent to hurt.
And as you ease along with the times,
Counting the years that you leave behind.
Quite often it is with an offence you are interrupted.
To be either punched, kicked, cut or bruised,
By an offender who is amused
To launch upon a victim unprotected.

You are often beaten, rubbed, raped or drugged,
And left in the street lying in your blood,
After being molested and viciously assaulted,
Or you may have been falsely arrested.
About to be jailed and tortured, hanged or shot,
And without knowing why or for what,
You have been so grossly offended.
Your life to be brutally forfeited,
And without ever knowing what wrong you did.

You are offended again and again,
And you have offended just the same.
In both cases sometimes amicably,
accidentally or deliberately.
And depending on which path you choose,
You end up sorry or amused,
By the results of your unworthy deeds.

You have offended at some time in your life,
Your father, your mother, your husband your wife.
Your son and your daughter, your brother and sister.
Your priest, your teacher and your employer,
Your friends and neighbours.
And you have offended complete strangers.

The ones you love and the ones you hate,
You have no rules, you don't discriminate.
And at times you just aggravate.
From your offences no one escapes.

You offend him simply because he is black,
Or for something or the other that you think he lacks.
Or because he is lazy, skinny or fat,
Or from his yard he chases your cat.
You offend him because he is white,
Or just because he got it right.
You offend him because he is wrong,
Or just because you didn't like what he had done.
Or simply because he is a Jew,
Or that he is a foreigner
and not one of you.

Or just because you don't like how he's dressed.
He needs a shave; he looks a mess.
And because he is after your daughter,
You don't want to see him set one foot near her.
So you offended him and warned him to keep away,
Or he would be sorry, a price he would pay.

You offended her just because she would not listen,
And marry for convenience, to become a citizen.
What does it matter if you don't love him?
He is fat and ugly, but he's got everything.

You offend her because she is ugly,
And when she is not,
You offend her because she is pretty.
And now you are offended
When a friend you trusted
Surprised you with what he did.

You are offended by your mum and your dad,
What they want you to do

is what makes you mad.
And sometimes by your brother and your sister too,
You are offended by what they do.
And by the stranger who took your car,
Beat you and raped you
and left you with scar.

You are also offended for your good deeds,
And quite often by the very ones you feed.
It doesn't really matter what you do,
Right or wrong, someone will offend you.

To be offended, as you already know,
is not a pleasant thing,
One is offended not only by you,
But by some of the things that nature brings.
You are offended by the sight of ugliness,
And by unpleasant taste and smell,
And by the fart that he lets go right in your face,
And then laughs at you as well.

You are offended by what has not been done,
And by what has not been said,
And by what has been done,
And what has been said as well.
For it is that very slip of your tongue,
That unlocks the door of hell.

You are offended within the law,
legally, justly and unjustly,
And quite often just as before,
both rightly and wrongly.
And with all the wrongs you have been offended,
Hardly ever are you compensated.
You are left wounded to suffer,
Whatever the consequences with you few bother.

And when it is by a deed that you are offended,
The hurt inflicted cannot be prevented.
And the degree of the pain is never the same,
As that which was intended.

Offensive deeds are many and numerous,
They are of a wide range of ways,
from the abominable to the ridiculous.
And they can be just trivial,
Like not attending your best friend's funeral.
Or being late and causing others an unnecessary wait.
Or they can be serious:
A thief broke into your home at Christmas.
Or with a gun, you threatened someone
Who became extremely frightened and nervous.
Some can be dangerous and destructive
When you offend with petrol and matches.
Sometimes they can also be very provocative,
If your sexual actions are too permissive.
They can also be comical and humorous,
Offensive jokes can make you happy or furious.
Some are intensely severe and detrimental,
Especially when they are committed by the law,
and they are legal.

To punish someone unjustly,
By the blatant abuse of your authority.
Or even when it has been done justly,
When you are innocent and they pronounced you guilty.

Yes, offences are not only executed in deeds,
And when in words,
they can drag you down to your knees.
They can make you cry,
Both inside and outside,
And they can pierce at your heart until it bleeds.

Offensive words as well as deeds – they both do hurt,
Deeds in the physical,
Like the rope that tightens around your throat.
Deeds in the psychological,
When you are paid a great deal less than what you are worth.
And the graffiti upon the wall
someone offensively wrote.

But words, unlike deeds, are only psychological,
And their agony is purely of the mental.
So a verbal offence is nothing more than a psychological matter,
And the remedy is yours,
and not of your doctor.
You do not need pills, tablets or any liquids,
A massage, plaster, or to be wrapped in bandages
What you do need of course is determination.
A very strong will, is an obligation.
You do not need any form of medicine,
Except, of course, a psychological lesson.

So give it a try and stop being hurt,
Smile to your offender and return with a joke.
Do not vituperate, and don't be aggressive,
Give no hint that you are offended,
In whichever way you have responded.

To disarm an offender is to leave him baffled,
When he sees that you're not offended,
he will be ruffled.
And when he is disarmed, he will be confused,
Not knowing what offensive words to use.
His weapons are now blunt instead of sharp,
He doesn't know with which words to cut you apart.
He is bewildered and left defeated,
His attack in words, will not be repeated.

Because they've lost their sharp edge,
they've lost their sting,
They could no longer hurt you, or anything.
They are useless words that can no longer offend,
Therefore, he has no further use for them.

Words can only hurt if you allow,
And they can be prevented if you know how.
Your response is triggered from deep in your mind,
And the words that hurt are so inclined.

So pull yourself together,
And try not to be offended
when you are called a nigger.
What is a nigger, and what does it mean?
Only that you are black,
and that is all, it seems.
So why be offended just because you are black?
Is it that you don't like the colour,
Or is it something much more than that?
Is it because of something you have
Or something you lack?
But whatever it is,
there is no need to crack.

You can pay no attention and take no heed,
Just don't be offended when called a half breed.
For what is a half breed, why are you so vexed?
When you are cut, you bleed just like the next.

Learn to smile and even laugh
When you are called a silly cow, or a calf.
Never get angry, whatever the name,
A collie, a bastard, do not be ashamed.
A hunky, a pummy, a stupid bitch, a witch,
A dirty yanky, a parky, you smell like fish.
A fat cow, an ugly owl.

Big nose, a bundle of dirty clothes.
They all may contain some sort of meaning,
And aimed at you to hurt your feelings.

But if you seize control and soften the landing,
You can prevent the offence of your exploding
And a vexation of spirit from erupting within you,
Bruising your feelings with colours black and blue.

There is no need to be offended,
because you are called old and grey,
If you want to live long,
that's a small price to pay.
And what is so wrong in being called fat and stupid?
As long as you are not caught
in deeds that are crooked.
You black bastard, you hunky face,
None of those words bear a mark of disgrace.
So pull yourself together, pull your socks up,
And to those silly words that offend you put a full stop.

But with words with damaging meaning supported by a
    deed,
It may not be as easy to control just how you feel.
Consider carefully the offensive word 'queer',
In its message it reveals
that you screw at the rear.
But then, if you think that is alright and good,
There is no need to be offended;
no reason why you should.

You asshole, you stinking dirty pig,
This is often in response to something awful you did.
You fucking bitch, you swine,
And so are those words, otherwise you are fine.
They are just retaliatory remarks
to express the anger you feel,

Aimed at the one who offended you
Either in his word or his deed.

You whore, you bloody liar, you thieving bastard,
You disgusting pervert –
Words of those kind, well, they are bound to hurt.
Because they associate you with a degrading deed,
Then it could be really hard
to control the vexation you feel.

Many an offence you take from words,
Are no more offensive than a punch on your nose.
Too often and unnecessarily you sulk and bother,
You cycle through life with a chip on your shoulder.
Taking offence very easily,
That any little silly joke
touches on your sensitivity.
When what was said, was meant only to be friendly,
And instead of laughing with the bloke,
You chose to be angry.

The grieving tears in your eyes you controlled successfully,
Likewise the stinking fart you let go, so sly and quietly.
You have learned to control your libidinous emotion,
With a burning desire for coition.
All these controls you handle successfully,
And yet at verbal remarks, you hurt so easily.

What is in a name that is so offensive?
Unless it associates you with something repulsive.
Sticks and stones can break your bones,
But names should never hurt you.
Unless, of course, they expose some distasteful thing you do.

So grab hold of yourself
and put your mind over matter,
If you do not mind, then it doesn't matter.

I am not saying that you will find this to be simple and
    easy,
Only that it could be done.
Just as you do, when you want to be strong.
So as you strengthen your muscles,
strengthen your will,
To ignore verbal offences
and a better life to live.
A rose by any other name is still a rose,
So with these last lines I shall close.
To offend someone is not a pleasant thing to do,
So don't you do unto others,
What you would not like to be done unto you.

Love, Like, Hate, Dislike

These are part of your natural feelings,
with discrimination expressed about
the things around you.
In choices you make,
you love, like, dislike or hate,
The things that you daily have to do.

Smell, taste, hear, see and feel,
Some things you reject,
others are to your appeal.
You either love, hate, like or dislike,
And your choice depends upon how you feel inside.
Love or like, hate or dislike,
Is how you feel about the things in your sight.

But how do you decide,
is it by some form of measure
Depending upon the gravity of your pleasure or
    displeasure?
How do you assess the differences in your feeling
Which you expressed in a verbal meaning?

You say that you love your wife,
and that you love your mother.
But your feelings are so different
for one and for the other.
You love your boyfriend,
your brother and your sister.
But your feelings are dislike
for your teacher and your neighbour.

You love whites and you hate blacks.
You love blacks and you hate whites.
Jews and foreigners,
you do not like their manners,
And you hate some of the things
they insist that are right.

You hate the government and what they are doing,
No money in your pocket and bad housing.
They tell you lies and to economise.
Vital services they are cutting.

So you love the workers when they are on strike,
It makes you feel good to see them unite.
But the pig-headed bosses,
you cannot stand their sight,
The way they treat the workers,
it's just not right.

You like your job and your boss,
But you hate people when they make you cross.
You hate arguments,
you cannot stand cruel experiments,
And you hate the place where you doss.

You like animals, birds, dogs and cats,
But you hate the squeaking of the rats.
Frogs and lizards you do not dislike,
But snakes and spiders they give you a fright.
Lions and tigers are fascinating,
You like to watch them when they are mating,
And at the moment of their kill.
But what you do not like
is the voracious sight,
As they devour to their fill.
Monkeys and chimpanzees, you'd like one as a pet,

Hens and peacocks you like to watch them fight to the
  death.
But pigs and cows you like to eat,
Their dismembered carcasses provide good meat.

You hate the piss that runs down his legs,
And onto the sheets on the bed it spreads.
You hate his breath, damn awful it smells,
But you love him dearly because he cares.

You like to peep through keyholes,
To catch a glimpse of her without her clothes.
And whatever else you can see,
Of the beauty of her nudity.
You like the gossips, whatever the news,
The more scandalous things be,
the more you're amused.
A joke and a laugh with someone to share,
And at whose expense? You don't really care.

You like to eat and you love a good meal,
But you prefer a woman with a sexy appeal.
For you to undress, love and caress,
You love to ejaculate,
but you hate the mess.

You love peanuts and ice-cream,
But you hate to splash out in a wet dream.
You love to travel, hang around and watch,
Foreign foods you don't like very much.

You love the grass when it is nice and green,
And a beautiful garden in a moonlit scene.
A night of romance, whenever you get the chance,
On the bank of a river, or near a stream.
You love jazz, a trip to Mars,
And the erotic maiden in your dream.

You love cricket and classical music,
And you have a craze for black magic.
You love flowers, midnight showers,
And a good romance lasting for hours.

You love the things that give you kicks,
Your scientific discovery,
The nude pictures in the art gallery.
Fast cars, women and booze,
You like to gamble, but hate to lose.

You love the kicks when you are flogged,
It makes you feel erotic,
and you jump like a frog.
You like the excitements,
the pangs and sensations,
And you love the whip
that lashes your frustrations.

You love danger because it makes you feel good,
It is exciting, and that is how it should.
You like to bully others
and to cause trouble whenever it suits you,
But you hate to be blamed
for the wrong things you do.

You hate law and order and discipline,
You like to be free to do anything.
You like to take chances, win or lose,
Making your own decisions, whatever you choose.

You hate unruliness and untidiness,
You hate a mess in general.
You hate sickness and disease,
And the irritation of people who are hard to please
And the nagging sounds of those depressed.

And the shouting and the quarrels of those who are vexed.

You like sports, football, cricket and all the rest,
And whenever you play,
you like to play at your best.
You like to win because you love the feeling,
Especially to hear the crowd cheering.

You love the excitement and the thrills,
A moment to forget about your bills.
You love Christmas and holidays,
And you like to do things in different ways.
You love a joke, you like to smoke,
But you hate the lump
that is stuck in your throat.

You like the erotic excitement of city life,
And dislike the placid surface of country life.
But you do not mind the country or the city,
It doesn't really matter,
as long as the people are friendly.

You like kids, although sometimes they make you mad,
Some naughty things they do,
they shame their mum and dad.
But you love them all the same,
It doesn't matter who is to blame,
A life without kids could be lonely and sad.

You love this and you love that,
You like to smile, and you love to chat.
And when you do not love or you do not like,
You either hate or dislike
something unpleasant which is in your sight.

But this assumption is not necessarily so,
With most things confronted,

there is another feeling you know.
That is a feeling of indifference,
You couldn't care a damn
about the sound, sight or the scent.
You neither love, like, hate or dislike,
You just couldn't care about the thing in your sight.

You hate poverty, filth and squalor,
Indecency and a life in the gutter.
You hate to see your children hungry,
You can't feed them because you have no money.
You hate to steal, even to get a meal,
And you hate the feeling when you are in need.

You hate heights and the darkness of the nights,
To be without a job and to be robbed.
You hate violence of any kind.
Though to be insulted, you don't really mind.
You hate learning,
you don't like to go to school,
You'd rather roam the streets and remain a fool.

You hate boys and you hate girls,
But you will love the boy who brings you pearls.
You love a romance burning with passion,
You love to feel the flame in every action.
And to perform without disturbance,
In your birthday suit,
which is still in fashion.

You love the thrills of her massage,
With her expert fingers romantically in charge.
You love her touches, so warm and sensational
They can only be described as exceptional.

You love a good day and a good night's sleep,
With a pillow at your head

And a lover's belly to warm your feet.
A pair of tits in the palm of your hands,
Making love without removing your pants.

You hate the sight of the fly drowning in your soup,
Don't know whether to give it the kiss of life,
Or just to flick it out with a scoop.
You hate carrots, corned beef and hard-boiled eggs,
But you love the men with hairy legs.

You hate the thought of growing old,
To lose your youth, perhaps even your soul.
You hate to be lonely
and to be dependent when you are old,
And to be a cripple and helpless
in a place damp and cold.
You hate those who insist that what you must do
Is always what you are told.
And you hate yourself,
because you have no wealth,
And you hate everybody in the whole wide world.

You hate yourself because you failed,
And because you are black,
or because you are pale.
And because you are poor.
You hate yourself,
but you don't know what for.

You hate to be told that you are stupid,
When the fact is, that you are a fool.
You like to think that you are not foolish,
Although you act like a jackass or a mule.

You love the picture,
and he likes the picture,
You dislike the picture

and he hates the picture.
And it is all but a matter of your feelings,
Which differ from you,
and from one to the other,
And by which each decides,
how much an object is appealing.

This feeling of choice which you embrace,
Is what you called your taste.
Which is frequently used and often abused
among the human race.
And not forgetting among other things,
The many choices you make
When buying and selling, and even judging.
Your decisions are based upon your taste.

But how else can you decide?
Whether or not you like the tie.
Whether a thing is bad or is it good,
Or it is ugly or very beautiful.
The song she sang, her beautiful tan.
The film you saw, the painted door.
The food you ate, the wine you drank.
The scent you smell in the place where you dwell.
Pictures, toys, wallpaper, curtains, cars,
Clothes, the colour of your ribbons,
And the winners you choose in competitions,
Guided by your taste,
is how you make your decisions.

It is decided by how much you liked it,
Whether it is a song, a film, a painting,
a new house, food, clothes or music.
It is not, for example, like a game,
Where physical results are the deciding thing.
And it has nothing to do with your feelings
So it is bound to be fair.

But when a decision is totally dependent
Upon your taste or your feelings.
The decision you made cannot be fair,
When you are the only one deciding
For what you like, someone else may hate,
And what you passed, someone else may fail.
So the more judges giving their opinion,
The better a chance of a fairer decision.
But hardly can a decision be totally fair,
When it depends upon your feelings,
the decision that you declare.

Because of the difference in your feelings and taste,
A winner could lose if the judge was replaced.
Love, like, dislike and hate
are just the expressions of a degree of your feelings
About the people or things you described as disgusting or
    appealing.
And from one stage to the other
Is your impartial sensitivity about anyone or anything
you reject or desire.
From the unbearable agony of pain,
To the exotic ecstasy of loving.
And so it is with everything in between,
Whether it is heard, felt, smelt or seen.

Often you make decisions for someone else,
You want to choose for them
what you like for yourself.
But whatever you recommend
emphasising that it's great
You should try and remember
that what you like, she may hate.

And that is what makes you say
that his taste is either good or bad,
Your taste may be better than his,

no reason to make him sad.
It is just a matter of your opinion,
which ought to be fully understood.
And you should not just use your taste to judge a thing
When you are only expressing your feeling.
But that will do if it only affects you,
But when it is for others,
you should heed their yearning.

Although it is true that many have taste similar,
Some are with excellent taste, and others inferior.
Choosing for yourself may still be better.
Making use of your individuality,
In matters of choice,
It is just a matter of your sensitivity.

When you tell a singer that she has won;
her song was the best,
It is simply your feelings which you have expressed.
But when you tell a tennis player that she has won,
Nothing to do with your feelings,
but actual points that count.
You tell a woman that she is beautiful,
she is lovely and very pretty,
How did you arrive at that decision,
by what authority?
It is simply your feelings you are expressing,
The sight of her to you
was most appealing.

Now consider the everyday choices you make.
They are of two categories, physical and mental,
And are of no other faith.
A physical decision expressing your choice,
Is a voluntary act, like using your voice.
You can do as you wish,
and perhaps whenever you wish,

You can leave it dirty,
or you can wash the dish.
You can act like a clown,
and you can sing a song.
Scratch your arse as you lie in the grass,
Something bites you as it goes past.
You can have a drink
if even you don't feel like it,
Read a book, prepare something to cook,
Make war, make love, or make a racket.

You can put on your clothes to have a shower,
Or take them off – whatever.
You can shout or shut your mouth,
Ride a bike, fly a kite and go out at night,
Wash your car, gaze at a star,
Or just sit on your arse wherever you are.

You can piss up the wall,
or give a friend a call,
A million things you can do,
And when they are but of the physical,
the choice is entirely up to you.
And the many things which you have done,
At a moment you can undo.
You can put your hat on and then take it off,
Reduce the pressure or apply more force.
You can run slowly and then run fast,
Or you can even stop to let someone pass.

So are your choices when they are of the physical,
They can be instantly repeated,
The choice is yours as you have decided.
You can do the same thing over and over again,
As long as you are not tired or suffering pain.

But when your choice is in the decisions you make

About people or things to love, like, dislike or hate,
You see, taste, smell, hear or feel,
And your senses respond to the appeal.
You love it or you like it,
and you say that it is the choice you make,
it may be your choice, and if it is,
Could you now choose to dislike it, or even hate?
The choice you have made is purely mental,
And it cannot be easily changed as it is with the physical.
It comes without a deed or an act to perform,
As like the piece of cloth, that you have torn.

A mental choice may be involuntary,
And to change swiftly from one state to the other
It just cannot be.
Take, for example, the chocolates you like,
Could you whilst eating them, hate them,
and then like them, and again hate them,
Then like them just as quickly as the pendulum swings from left to right?

You can shut and open your eyes momentarily,
Could you hate and then like the same picture just as quickly?
Take a person, for that matter –
Could you love her and then hate her,
and again love her and then hate her
Without a change in her or your attitude or behaviour?

You cannot switch a mental choice
as you do with a physical choice;
Now you see it and now you don't;
Now you love it and now you don't.
You have no control of your feelings,
And you cannot hate what is to you most appealing.
For such a choice is involuntary.
It is not the same as talking to somebody.

It is all to do with the nature of your sensitivity,
And what you like, you cannot just hate instantly.
That is how things are,
that is your nature,
And that's how it will be forever.

But a change in your feelings could appear,
You can hate what you did love
and like what you did hate.
But only in response to a change which has taken place.
You now dislike something you once did like,
Because of a change which no longer appeals to your sight.
Or a change which is now not to your taste,
You don't like the meal they put on your plate.

You can also control your feelings to like or to hate,
And often it is done to acquire a taste.
By regular efforts you do undertake,
And it is achieved after some time,
Depending upon the power
or the state of your mind.
Eventually you acquire a taste,
For the very thing that you once did hate.

Physical and mental choices really differ,
And it is easy enough to tell one from the other.
You love or like, dislike or hate,
In response to your feeling's dictates
To whatever you may hear, touch, smell or see,
All this depends upon your sensitivity.
And the feelings triggered from within your mind,
Are simply the responses genetically inclined.

A mental choice is a genetic command,
To which you respond hand in hand.
It is entirely involuntary,
A fact of life for you and everybody.

It is this form of choice which made you different
From the many people wherever you went.
Or you may just as well love what everybody loves
And hate what everybody hates,
As you can so easily do in the physical choices you make.

So this you ought to remember,
That your mental choice is not a voluntary behaviour.
It is merely responses from the influences within.
The will of your mind
is like the will of a king.

Consider the habit known as an addiction,
It could be described as an involuntary choice
gone completely out of hand.
You cannot refrain, no matter how hard you try,
And after you have committed,
you ponder and wonder why.

This is the same for the drug addict,
The smoker and the alcoholic,
And of course, the homosexual.
His sexual choice, like yours, is mental.
And because this is so, he has no control.
Without a determined effort,
he will do as he is told,
Obeying the commands from within his mind.
His genetic disorder, to him it is unkind.

And this is what it is all about,
When you say that you like, dislike, hate or love.
Your emotions or feelings for people and things,
Are simply the responses, of your senses,
to your genetic blueprints.

Sleeping Demons

What are they, where are they, the sleeping demons?
Behind you, in front of you, or all around you?
Deep down inside you is where they lay,
Like the silent crocodile awaiting its prey.
And when in an instant a demon is disturbed,
In a rage it awakes to pursue its goal.

A demon in you is now awakened,
And a feeling within you is immensely heightened.
To the pulsating rhythms of your heartbeat,
The name of this demon is 'Conceit'.

And so you have become overwhelmed with pride
To such an extent that you cannot hide
The joy in your soul,
the joy in your smile.
You are proud of what you have done,
And you are proud of the honour that you have won.
Or proud of something that others have done,
And proud of the honour that they have won.

A friend, your father, your mother, your son,
Your family, your team, your school, your nation.
You are proud because among them you belong,
And when you are with them you feel as one.
So you are proud of what they have achieved,
And the honour that they have received.
You are proud to be a partner,
To be the father or the mother.
Of such gifted children,

It is so wonderful to be with them.

You rise from rags to riches,
Through difficulties, tribulations and hitches.
A self-made man, you do whatever you can,
And often with the help of the missis.
So of your wife you are very proud,
Although she nags, and sometimes too loud.
But you know that she is a very good wife,
A woman for keeps, the whole of your life.
Because whatever she does,
she makes you proud.

Too proud to speak first and make up
Whenever you quarrel and break up,
You are sorry inside,
without her you would die.
You don't want to lose him,
To you he means everything.
And yet from each other,
behind your pride is where you hide.

You are proud also of the things you have got,
A successful business, a mansion, a yacht.
Horses, a title and a stamp unique,
A pension fund, jewels and some antiques.
You are very proud also of the people you meet.
And when it is for them that decisions you make,
You feel really proud when things turn out great.

Yes, you are proud of what you are,
Your success in life as a famous star.
White or black as chalk or tar,
But some failures in life come through this colour bar.

Yes, you are proud that you have made it
From the slime of the gutters, to be a favourite.

And through the barriers of hate and prejudice
You climbed to the top
from the bottom of the precipice.

Proud to be in the freemasonry,
And a distinguished member of high society.
And as a member of the Klu Klux Klan,
White supremacy is for what you stand.
Proud of your killings, burnings and shootings,
And of the lynchings you do, whenever you can.

You said that you were proud even to be a homosexual,
Because your sodomy is now legal.
And there is no need to hide your face,
Your sexual perversions are no disgrace.
So you can be a prime minister,
A judge, a general, or a film star,
And screw the arsehole of your partner,
And tell the whole world that you are proud.

So proud of yourself and scared of the truth,
You live a life of a lie,
in a neat and smart suit.
You pretend that you care,
and treat the people unfair,
Just like the rest of those thieving brutes.

Too proud to say no or even yes,
When your support is needed at someone's request.
You would not accept a helping hand,
Just because that help is from a woman
Or from someone you considered inferior,
Because of his station, his colour or culture.

Too proud to refrain from a challenge,
Although you know that you have no chance.
So you thrust your faith into providence's hands,

Too proud to hesitate or to run away,
So you face the dangers, come what may.
Even your death you would face,
But you are too proud to confront disgrace.

Too proud and independent-minded.
With your pride your eyes are blinded.
You would not listen to any reason.
Pride is the venom in your head which is swollen.
You cannot think straight;
you are nothing but a fake.
You want to have and to eat your cake.

Too proud to admit that you have failed,
Your head was too big, and your courage quailed.
Because of your pride, yourself you denied,
Many opportunities that were worthwhile.
And you later regret,
the opportunities you let
Slip through your fingers and go by.
And then to face the reality,
The torments of disgrace in bankruptcy,
Behind a smile you try to hide your feelings,
No one must know that inside you are bleeding.
You will rather die, and let them wonder why.
Your wound was never really healing.

And now that your pride is wounded and severely hurt,
You tend to get the desire
to put a knife to your throat.
Because you are too proud to face the world,
Suicide's bid has become an inspiring goal.
But then you found another way,
And the wounded demon in you has ended its play
To crawl miserably back to its sleep,
You then swallow your pride, burying it deep.
And no sooner that this is done,

Up pops another awakened demon.

It is the demon of anger and the demon of hate.
Sometimes they are together,
like the icing on a cake.
And so inflamed and violent are your feelings,
With the poisons of hate and anger in your veins.
You get so touchy; you are always angry,
With a friend, the family, or just anybody.

And from your anger out creeps your hate,
Aimed at a relative, a neighbour or a mate.
You are very angry sometimes for trivial things,
You hate your friend just because she wins.

Angry sometimes, yes, for a very good reason,
As being falsely arrested and sent to prison.
Or because of your job that you have lost,
And your life style it has cost.
And because your wife has left you.
Saddened and depressed,
you don't know what to do.
You just cannot satisfy a woman,
You are impotent, and can't get an erection.

Angry because you had won the pools,
But you forgot to post your coupon,
So two million pounds is what you lose.
And now back to the kitchen in your apron.

Angry because you were jilted; your house burgled,
And your daughter molested.
Your brand new car has been stolen;
You have been beaten up, and your nose is broken.
Angry because you missed the train,
Or because it was late again.
And because you lost the election,

No point in being a defeated politician.

And as you feel outraged in anger,
It transforms into a hate with flames of fire.
So you become more and more angry
And so often unnecessarily.
You get angry for no cause at all,
With Tom, Dick or Harry
and even with Paul.

And you hate yourself and everybody,
As the demons in you get stir crazy.
And in their madness other demons awake,
And strangle your sanity, you behave inappropriate.
Anger, hate, jealousy and envy,
Those are the demons now in control of your body.

So you become jealous of him and of her,
Always it is of someone you know.
Your neighbour, a business partner, a friend or a foe.
And often it is of a close acquaintance,
You are jealous about some flaming romance.

You are jealous about love affairs,
She has left you with your heart in tears.
And gone with another for whom she cares.
And now you are hideously jealous.

Jealous because your friend had intercourse,
And you have never had it yet.
He got on the job,
whereas you were snubbed,
And almost by everyone you had met.
You are jealous of his success,
Songs, wine, women and the rest,
That aroused your temper with raging envy.
And you are jealous because

she won and you lost,
And for revenge you are desperate and hungry.

You thought that you had won,
Because you felt that you sang the best song.
Now you are jealous, envious and bitterly angry.
You are jealous because she is very pretty,
She is always so nice, charming and friendly.
She knows how to talk, she's got a sexy walk,
And she gets along fine with everybody.

You're jealous because your friend got married
And you may be left on the shelf.
This always happened so now you are worried,
Whether you will ever find someone else.

And when you are jealous or possessed by envy,
It is of a friend or someone in the family.
You are hardly ever jealous of a stranger,
Your feelings are indifferent
and so is your behaviour.
You are jealous of your sister,
and when you are not,
You envy your brother for what he has got.
His possession of material things
Transmits envious waves right through your brains.

You are jealous or envious of someone else,
When things with you are not going as well.
And when those feelings snatched hold of your soul,
That's when the demons in you are in full control.
Your jealousy and your envy then intensify,
And that's when you go crazy, and act unwise.
To the demons in you,
you become their tool,
In behaviour intolerable
and that of a fool.

And no sooner a demon returns to its sleep,
Awake is another to plunge you deep
Into the gutters of lust and vice,
Where your emotions are swamped by a plague of lice
And if you are not poisoned by their disease.
Other demons in you cause you unease.

As they chained and dragged you upon their track,
Where selfishness and prejudice,
malice and bitchiness,
In you they stack.
And someone becomes a victim to your displeasure,
The depth of their adversity
hardly can you measure.
So you continue, urged on by the demons in you,
Someone unlucky is at the mercy of what you do.

You want to keep it all,
not a bit to give,
You couldn't care a damn
if he'll die or live.
So because of your selfishness
someone nearly dies,
To show a little gratefulness
was too much for your hide.
Blinded by your bitchiness,
you accused him with a lie,
Your wrath was full of wickedness,
no one can imagine why.

Influenced by your prejudice,
you robbed him of a job,
His rights and privileges,
you denied him with a snub.
And maddened by your prejudice,
like a rabies-infected dog,
You plunged upon a stranger

with intent to assault and mug.
And when you are not prejudiced,
You feel an urge for malice.
And woe unto him or unto her
Who stands in your way wherever you go.

Because trailing with you are the evil vibrations,
To which you respond,
like a puppet to the demons.
Which influence your emotions whenever they are awake,
And you be damned by the actions you do undertake.

Demons in you are better left asleep,
To spare you from being emotionally weak
And to save yourself from ever becoming prey.
Ruthless demons in you,
it's on your feelings they play.

Five Bridges to Cross

Your five bridges to cross.
From your beginning to your end,
There are five bridges to cross.
But where are they, who can tell?
Are they over the waters between heaven and hell?
And each with its own length of time
To take you across your pentagon,
Shaped with injustice, vice and crime.
From your arrival and until you depart.
A short period that seems a lifetime,
from beginning to end.
But how many of you do get across,
Whether alone or with a friend?

Your entire journey is for you to complete,
Regardless of the obstacles you frequently meet.
How many of you do make it to the end,
Without collapsing half way
at a corner or a bend?
How many of you do stop on your way,
And right where you stop
you lie down and stay?

You can vanish from your first bridge, number one,
And sometimes even before your journey is begun.
Slowly you came, but swiftly you go,
And without even finding out
Some of the things that you should know.
Such as knowing your name,
Or from where, how, or why you came.

And you do not even know,
which man is to blame,
Or the woman who suffered all the pain.

And that was because you were just a babe,
Most times you were carried or you were laid.
You slept or cried right where you lay,
Until your needs were attended and then you smiled.
Nothing you did for yourself,
But to fart, piss, shit and belch.
And if it had been up to you,
Even those things you would have paid someone to do.

But you soon got fed up with that life style,
And you began to crawl to the things nearby
Not knowing yet what to do.
So you played with fire,
nothing was a danger,
And your napkin you used as a loo.

You crawled upon your knees for many months,
As though reaching out for the end.
And when you smiled as if it was the end you had found,
It turned out to be just another bend.
And when you got tired of crawling,
you learned to walk and to run.
And no sooner had you learned to run,
The fun of your journey had begun.

So you hurried along, not knowing
Exactly where you were going,
Your bridge it seemed too long.
You then stopped and gazed,
You looked back and waved,
And caught a breath of air.
Then you turned around and carried on,
Where you were heading?

You neither knew nor cared.

And just when you are having lots of fun,
You can talk, walk and off you run.
To wash your hands as you clean your bum,
You find that you are but a babe no more.
You came through the beginning
and now you reached the end,
Your first bridge crossed and every bend.
You are now on a different shore.

Time has taken you across,
Nothing you remember and nothing you've lost
Upon another bridge for you to cross.
Not as a babe, but now as a child,
And upon this bridge you can run wild.
You soon discovered that it is great fun to play,
So you want to do so every day.

It is your time for lots of fun,
You couldn't care a damn if it is snow or sun.
It is a wonderful time of your life,
You have no bills, no husband, no wife.
You have no worry of any kind,
You are clothed, fed and sheltered,
and your worries are mine.
Your only problem is that you have to learn,
And it seems a burden of great concern.

But at least you make a lot of friends,
Life's a paradise you hope will never end.
Presents at Christmas and at birthdays too,
Everyone giving and no one takes from you.
Everyone willing with a helping hand,
Though sometimes annoying,
they wouldn't give you a chance.
Grandma, grand-dad, mum and dad,

They wouldn't leave you for a minute –
they often drive you mad.

And as you raced along your bridge step by step,
You learned to be careful of the people you met.
You learned on your bridge there are many dangers,
Slowly crawling by are many child molesters.
You learned to be aware of cunning strangers.
They are hidden in disguise, but are child slavers.
Like a snake in the grass,
They await your pass,
and strike their deadly poison.
And if you are caught unaware,
They will persuade you of how much they care,
Until your fragile heart they have stolen.

You are at an age most vulnerable,
And you can be hurt by people most dishonourable.
So as you trot along making tracks,
Be careful of the rot and the cracks.
Always follow your parents' code,
And do not ignore what you are told.

Your second bridge is long and slippery,
Many of its dangers are due to trickery.
So remember that you are just a child,
And to safely cross you will need a guide.
You have just started,
and still have a long way to go,
So don't be too excited,
or an ill wind may blow
And lift you up, and drop you down
From off your bridge to under the ground.

So don't you ever try to cross alone,
But to helping hands from strangers,
you must not be prone.

Or you may be scalded or severely burnt,
There are many lessons that must be learnt
To safely cross your bridge.

And as soon as have you got used to things,
Playing freely, enjoying your games
Without any worries, like the bird that sings.
At the end of your bridge you flap your wings,
And make ready to get across.

As a child you just couldn't wait
To get quickly across to the other gate.
You were always ever so very anxious
To be on the other side you just felt you must.
And now that you are safely near,
You pause in thought and with a stare.
Just a few more steps and you will be there.
Much more exciting is the life over there,
So you hasten to the end.

Now one more step and you are across
The waters of innocence which have washed your sores.
You have stepped upon your other bridge
Where the waters beneath are filled with sewage
The challenge is that you should not fall,
Into the sewage or you shall lose all.

Here is a new life for you to begin,
On this bridge you can do many more things.
You have no doubt it will be interesting
The sort of life you intend to be living
Now as a teenager, and to be responsible
For your own behaviour.
And other things that you ought to be able to do,
Without someone doing them for you.

This is a bridge of tremendous pressure,

Both from society and from nature.
On this bridge you prepare for your future,
And more than any time before.
The pressure of learning is tremendous,
Plus other pressures which are dangerous.
You are trained and you learned something,
By means of which you will earn your living.
In a field of your choice of vocation,
That may secure you from the pangs of starvation.
You have to learn to make decisions
And be responsible for your actions.
You have to learn to say no or yes
Without getting yourself in a hell of a mess.

It is on this bridge
That your friends mostly influence you
They very often try to persuade you what to do.
Join in their gang and shoplift,
Or in a crowd to pick a pocket.

Or have some booze or a smoke,
Or as you like, you can have them both.
Or take off her dress and have some sex,
That's what it's for, no one will be vexed.
You cannot resist the temptation for a taste of honey.
The urge is so strong,
And you are in love with somebody.

You are on the bridge most vulnerable to temptations,
In matters of booze, and smoke,
Sex and friendship obligations.
It is on this bridge you fantasise most about love and sex,
And often get yourself tangled in a hell of a mess.
You are split between yourself and your parents,
What could you do without their interference?

But they know the strength of the forces of temptation,

That requires a very strong will,
The careful thinking and cautious decisions'
That require wisdom and skill.
They know of the pros and cons,
The dangers of building on volcanic grounds.
They know the treachery of quicksand,
That drags you down the moment you stand.
They know the silence of the deadly serpent,
And the whistling of a perilous wind
And the powers of the gushing waters,
Lashing to draw you in.

So they want to guide you,
But you don't want to be guided,
Because you consider yourself able-minded.
You want to find out for yourself
The dangers on your bridge
And everything else.
You do not want to listen to advice,
Or to do as you are told.
You'd rather be cut and bruised, break a bone
And freeze out in the cold.

You are trapped in a conflict all the time.
Your will persuades you not to toe their line.
So you harden in your determination
To do what is to your satisfaction.
Until into trouble you landed yourself
With a child you cannot handle,
And there is no one else.

Then suddenly you found
That the teenager's bridge is not so long.
It is a place for very hard work,
With a little fun and some jokes.
It is the bridge where you make great preparation,
For your life ahead after graduation.

And that life depends upon how well you prepared,
Somehow it determines the comfort of your bed.

And when your preparations are all over
A teenager you are but no longer.
So that bridge you reluctantly leave behind,
And upon the other you confidently climb.
Unto the bridge for adults,
Where you take with you all your skills and your faults.
You pause and smile presumptuously,
Inside you is the feeling that you are now ready
To step outside and face the world
Whatever the weather, sunshine, wind and rain, or freezing cold.

You are now upon a bridge that is very long,
Slippery and dangerous with ups and downs.
Paved with disappointments and opportunities,
Burdens, problems and responsibilities,
You either straighten your back or you bend your knees
To carry the weight of your duties.

For upon this bridge you are a man,
And when you are not, you are a woman.
But whatever you are, there is romance,
So get yourself a partner and drop your pants.

Upon this bridge with a partner you mate,
Whom you lustfully loved and then later hate.
It is on this bridge where you multiply,
Or you can add, but do not divide.
The seeds you sow to blossom
Remain buried in the dirt; there are always some.

It is on this bridge you have to work.
A living to earn is not a joke.
You are burdened daily with a cross

Which you have to carry on behalf of your boss.
And there are commitments to your family,
To clothe and prevent them from being hungry.

And upon this bridge you are mostly scared,
Afraid of the day you may lose your bread.
Afraid of the bills you cannot pay
That may lead to your house being taken away.

Afraid for the ones you dearly love.
Something may strike them from above.
Snakes, scorpions and spiders,
Loan sharks, thieves and bloodsuckers,
Slavers, exploiters and murderers.

This is the bridge full of crime and vice,
And cheats who gamble with loaded dice.
The bridge whereupon you can lose or win,
A fortune, your wife, your life, or everything.
And as you proceed thereupon,
Piranhas in the water,
Vampires in the air,
Tigers and lions on the ground.

It is a bridge infested with dangers,
From the woodlice in the crannies,
To the strangers around corners.
The spider in the grass, creeping up your arse,
Blackmailers and traitors,
And bullying evil-doers wherever you pass.
The shadows in the night
That disturbed your sleep,
The footsteps of a thief
That made the floorboards squeak.
Danger in your house and with a stranger or a friend,
And among those upon whom you depend.
And below your bridge it is dangerous too,

Rough waters gushing up to swallow you.
Danger among dangers
And danger in your pleasure,
Your life is full of dangers
From man and from nature.

And despite all the dangers,
The decisions are yours,
Carefully to be implemented
And in compliance with the laws.

It is upon this bridge
You mature and develop,
The widening of your experiences
Hardly ever stops.
Trials and tribulations,
Upon your door they knock.
Success or distress is what your key can unlock.

It is upon this bridge
Where you rise or fall,
High up in the sky,
Or beneath them all.
This is the bridge where you accumulate
Wealth, fame and prosperity,
Or just a silver plate.
This is the bridge where you are always too busy;
You cannot find even a little time,
To be with your family.
You are always out there making money,
Or at a meeting with somebody.

This is the bridge where you need to prepare,
For life on the other side,
Where you may be in need of good care.
And that you may not have any cause to regret
When things are not

As you were led to expect.

This is the bridge where you meet with the end
Of your lifetime's work, to enter retirement.
It is a sad feeling that accompanies you across,
You feel as though your whole life's work
Is now completely lost.
Completely stripped of your power and glory,
Now that you have lost all your authority.
And you can feel like a complete jackass,
Taken down from your high horse
To sit on the grass.

But for others the feeling is just great,
At last comes the end of a job
Which they grew to hate.
The end of a life's long boring routine,
Which had caused them much suffering in between.
And now for a life full of leisure,
Which they hope to live out with great pleasure.
To rise in the morning at any time
Without the worries of being late,
And then to be treated disrespectfully unkind.

On this bridge you have all the time in the world,
You can spend it idly,
Or do some of the things that you should have done.
You are delighted now that you are a grandparent,
But you regret that you can no longer get pregnant.

Grey on your head, on your face, and in your pants;
Everything is grey, even your romance.
And when you are not grey,
It is because you are bald,
Your sexual drive is misfiring
Or it is completely stalled.

On this bridge most things you can no longer do,
Your taste and your craze have changed in you.
This is the bridge where you are often left alone,
Family and friends are no longer concerned.
You could be lonely more than any other time in your life,
And you can lose your privacy
More than you had ever lost with your husband or your
    wife.

You are old, wrinkled and feeble,
Senile to the extent that you are not able.
And as you continue to drag yourself along,
In each step you weaken, instead of being strong.

Drifting slowly towards your end,
Hands shaking, and your backbone bent.
Your time is nigh for recompense.

And as you take but just one more look at your life,
From this your last bridge you leap
To your hell or your paradise.
Your five bridges you have crossed;
Your journey is completed.
Your book is closed, your task is ended
And now at last, you are terminated.
From where you came you may now return,
To claim your place in the unknown.

Natural Segregation

Well, now that you are aware,
Of this phenomenon that is only quite clear.
Within the society wherever you are,
Alone, with a friend or your family,
In a place near or far.
You have five bridges to cross.

And upon your bridge you encounter many,
And with a number of people you become friendly.
And to a few, very closely attached,
In a friendship with common interest
This is a friendship well matched.

Your bridge, your perilous place of abode,
Where either upon your knees you creep,
Or you hustle upon your broad flat feet,
Or drag yourself towards your end to meet,
In a resting place deep underneath.
It is determined by your age.
And not until you cross over
From one bridge unto the other,
And secure your burdens upon your shoulder,
Then you can turn to another page.

You hustle and you bustle and you become weary.
And as you sit down to rest you feel lonely.
So you gear up into search for company,
To talk and to laugh with somebody,
And without even leaving your boundary,
It is right on your bridge where you remain.

Because your bridge is the place where you belong,
And it is there that all your friends are found.
And not upon the bridges you have already left,
Nor the ones some distance beyond.
And when you want to be a bit more segregated,
Then you choose from among the sex
To which you are related.

Undoubtedly you would hardly ever choose
A friend from another bridge
Unless it is someone you would conveniently use.
Is there some reason that you could explain
When you want a friend to play a game?
Why you do not move from bridge to bridge
And make friends with people of any age?
Why don't you associate with anyone,
Making good friends as you go along?

Why doesn't a child make friends with an adult,
The fact that he doesn't, is it his fault?
Why doesn't the teenager choose friends old and grey,
Or with kids half his age, he decides to play?
Why do girls choose girls and boys choose boys?
And the same is to be said about adults.

What is the reason, what laws do you obey
That with your age and your sex is where you always
    choose to stay
What guides you, what prompts you,
An instinct right or wrong,
With people your age and your sex,
Among them is where you feel you belong.

And this is a true phenomenon
Of your natural segregation,
Each with their age and their sex in a separation.
And it is not even forced upon you legally,

But something you respond to naturally.
And it is with them that you feel entirely at ease,
Knowing that you can now do almost anything that you
  please.
You can say most of the things that you wouldn't otherwise
  say,
And even do some naughty things whilst you joke and play.

You know that you can laugh, cry and converse,
Have a fight, rub noses and feel real close.
You can exchange secrets, because you trust one another,
Share your sweets, your booze, your cigarettes,
In giving and taking from each other.
You can do anything, likewise say anything,
And it really doesn't matter.
When you are among friends,
You do them together.

That is when you know
That you are in the right company,
Which is not the same
With your mummy and your daddy.
Friends and parents are not the same.
With your friends you can play any sort of game.
But there are many things that you would not say or do
When your parents are with you.
So you can still feel a bit lonely
When you are with your parents,
And this is because of your age difference.

So it is from your bridge where best you choose,
Someone your age with whom to piss and booze.
Someone your sex who would not be vexed,
Someone, in some way, is something like you.

And it is by this action,
Making your selection,

Whereby you do segregate.
And quite often, the friend you have chosen
Is like yourself in many ways.
So if you are Black, you mix with Blacks,
And if you are a Jap, you mix with Japs.
If you are White, you'd rather mix with Whites,
A Jew with Jews, an Indian with Indians,
An Arab with Arabs, and a Muslim with Muslims.

To segregate is an instinct of your peremptory nature,
To which you respond,
Discriminatory in your behaviour.
To attach yourself to some group or the other,
By virtue of your age, your sex or religion,
Your language, race or colour
Or your social status and common interest,
Physical fitness or your culture.
And in some cases, in different places,
It may even go a few steps further.
The style of your dress,
Your hat or your hairdo,
By which you are recognised
As a skinhead, a priest, a punk, a monk, or a zulu.

It is always something which guides you to determine
Your preference in choosing your mates or your friends.
And you are never really conscious or aware of the fact,
That in your choice you have committed a segregation act.
You simply want to be with people like yourself,
Those who fulfil your natural criteria,
And to hell with anyone else.

It is those differences,
And particularly your age and your sex,
Your race and language, your culture and colour,
That form the tight knots
That tie a people securely together.

As with the flocking birds of the same feather,
When you are among your kind
You feel a great deal better.

You don't step up and make friends with just anyone,
Knowing quite well that you don't belong.
Because he is not your age,
Nor does he speak the same tongue,
He is not one of you,
So you simply move on.

It is for yourself a companion you seek,
So you tend to be particular and somewhat discreet.
If you are rich, then your friends are rich;
And if you are poor, your friends too are poor.
But when you become rich, you want them no more.
If you are literate, your friends are literate,
And if you are illiterate, your friends are illiterate.
Always in some way or the other you do segregate
From those around you who do not fit.

In your need to be with somebody,
like yourself, with whom to be friendly.
You make contact with people within your environment,
Segregating yourself unintentionally,
This is a fact you cannot prevent.
No matter how hard you try
And it happens wherever you went
No need for you to ask why
Take the alcoholic or drug addict –
And consider them for instance.
It is drugs or booze they will prefer
Instead of a good romance.
Likewise there is the queer.
Among homosexuals he feels a very welcome atmosphere.
Because in this act you find your equals
With whom you feel they do care.

And when you smoke, you are always ready to share.
Take the child prodigy, he is exceptional,
And that is why he is lonely –
Hardly ever can he find an equal
Someone like himself, for good company.

You cohere with those who share
Your views, your desires and your faults,
But as a child among children,
And an adult among adults.
You seek your company not with anybody,
But from among those upon your bridge,
And so your first step in natural segregation is taken,
When you choose a companion, someone of your age,
Your sex, race, culture, colour and other qualities,
For a good friendship, they are the seeds
From which common interest makes the grouping feasible,
Therefore choosing to mix with people like yourself
Is highly understandable.

You do segregate by remaining within the group to which you belong,
And without a thought of whether it is right or wrong.
Just as the sun is separated from the moon,
So is man from woman,
And only by the wall in a single room.
And so too are the young from the old
By the many years of experience,
In weathers hot and cold.
And by your wrinkles and your greys,
Which inform the young that you are not of their age.
And even by your sexual drive:
When you are eighty,
You do not marry someone who is twenty-five.

Natural segregation is a daily practice
Among males and females of all ages

And it is without bias or malice.
It can be seen everywhere,
Among all the people out there.
And it could be seen right within
Institutions, churches, schools, or any building.

It is performed by you and yet you cannot see
That it is the base for a good company.
It is with you and for all your life,
Natural segregation is a temperament that is wise.
Because of the difference of your thinking and your views,
Influenced by your age, your sex, your culture,
And even by the language you used.

You cannot just associate with anybody,
So to segregate is the move that comes naturally.
With some group or the other,
There's always one where you belong,
And by your natural instincts,
Your place will be found.

A Sharing Need

This need within you dwells
Like the unquiet waters of a well.
It is simply another flow
From the reservoir you already know,
Namely, your mother nature.

And it is like the many others,
Which are in the nature that is yours.
And conspicuous in your behaviour.
To share is a burning desire
Within you, and without flame or fire.
It is a strong irresistible urge
For a companion to emerge.
It is a prevailing human need
To be with someone is how you feel.

To divide the things you have to do
With a helping hand given to you.
And the things you have gathered in your keep,
Whether just a few or many, expensive or cheap.
Whether they are valuable or just ornamental,
Whether they are priceless or sentimental.
Or whether they are of no value at all,
Something big or something small.
In your heart you feel the joy whenever you share.

Because depression you have defeated
And rejection you have unseated.
And the feeling of being alone
With thoughts that are no one's concern.

And yourself you have set free
From the prison for the miserly.

To share is to give, and without so doing,
Then what kind of a life would you be living?
So that is why, with someone you will share your life.
Be it a lover, a husband or a wife,
A friend or a relative,
The objective is the same,
To take and to give.
For nature herself has designed it so,
To love is to share with someone you know.
So with your family you share a home,
Or your life is lonely living alone.

You live your life for your family,
A load of responsibilities is what you carry.
It is a life of love and care,
Inspired by the many things you share.
Your problems, your worries, your ups and downs,
The joys and the sorrows of rights and wrongs.
The smiles, laughs and quarrels,
The farts you smell,
And the used bath towels.
The shower with your lover,
And your dirty bath water.
Your shirt, your shoes,
Your tie and your knickers,
Your boots, your comb,
Your tooth-paste and pyjamas.
Your book, your pen, whatever you have,
Even the aggravation of your bad manners.
Your thoughts, your dreams and your feelings,
When they are shared,
That's when life is worth living.

You do numerous things

And often for yourself,
For your family and your friends
And for strangers as well.
But there are many things you cannot do alone,
And when things are shared
The seeds of goodwill are sown.

This is evident in your society
In the need for someone in everybody.
Each to their responsibilities
Is how you earn your bread,
These are the pillars of society,
The path on which you are led.

And whenever we are together,
With each performing their path,
Burdens are divided and shared,
Right from the very start.
And so with many hands together,
They make work shorter and lighter.
Nothing could have been better
To make things feel just right.

You drink a beer and have a meal
When you are alone. How does it feel?
You sit by yourself with no one to chat,
So with the birds you share your snack.
Or behind a book you hide your face,
To escape your loneliness,
In the story you embrace.

You walk alone and then you pause,
To think why you are lonely;
What is the cause?
And with your thoughts you wrestle and you struggle,
but you can't find the answer in the hassle.

So with your lonely eyes,
You gaze upon the skies,
In a manner accusing,
Not with truth but with lies.
And then you looked upon the muddy waters,
In the quiescent river nearby,
Searching for a friendly shadow,
But deep down in the mud it hides.
And upon your weary face,
You wear a deceiving smile,
To cover the traces of your loneliness
That pierce right through your eyes.

A piece of a cake and a cup of tea,
Caviare and champagne you shared with nobody.
But what does it matter how pretty you are
When your heartbeats are lonely,
Without joy or pleasure.

Life is to share, and sharing is rewarding.
It puts a smile on a face and joy within.
For when you have and some you give,
It is not wrong, but is the right way to live.
Although less you will have in whatever things,
Joy in your soul is your principal gain.
And the more that you share,
Your reward is greater,
As if it was multiplied over and over.

But when ever you are filled with love and all you keep,
With it buried in your heart, or under your feet
You would not share with anyone you meet,
Then your life must be dull and rather bleak.

And so it is the same with material things,
Whether you be a millionaire, a billionaire,
Or a king of kings.

When before nature you are all the same.
You need a smile and a joke
And a laugh to share with a bloke.
You need a cuddle and love
And understanding hearts,
Someone to play with
And even in a game of darts.

You feel pain, hunger and thirst like anyone else,
And when you are choked up with wind,
You either fart or belch.
You can be happy in someone's company,
Or on your own, be miserable and lonely.
You can share or hoard it all,
Possessions of material things only
Is a life worthless, boring and dull.

So who wants to be a millionaire?
If with all you have,
You have no one to share.
No one to share your roof,
A piece of cake or a loaf.
No one with you to share a joke,
No one with you to share a coke.
No one to hold your hand,
Not even to say, yes I can.
No one to say, I am very sorry,
And for you who would really worry.
With no one to share the sun,
The moon and the stars, or just a song.
Or the rainbow that is painted in the sky,
Or the tears that fill your eyes.
Or the joys that come with a smile.
You have so much and yet you cannot buy,
Just a little bit of happiness,
Peace of mind and forgiveness.
Nothing for you to share,

With someone who really cares.

Who wants to be a billionaire?
When all you have are banks of money,
Big mansions, jets and loads of worry.
No wife, no children, no family.
And with no one a single thing to share,
No one to love who really can care,
No one when needed who will be there.
No one to share your bed,
To warm your heart and relax your head.
And who won't even care if you're alive or dead,
No one for you who'd shed a tear.

Now who wants to be a royal king?
If you can't find someone to take your ring.
No one who wants to be royal,
If it means they will have to be loyal.
No one with you to share a fling.
Or your empire with everything.
Your truths and your lies and your secrets.
No one to share your royal biscuits.

Who wants to be rich and lonely?
With no friends or family.
With pockets loaded and a heart that is empty,
Nothing you can share with anybody.
But what does it matter; who cares?
To be very rich and with no one to share,
No one to love and no one to care.
Then in spirit you are miserably poor,
And with all your wealth
You can't heal your sore,
Nor stop loneliness knocking your door.
Your solitary heart can't find a cure.

Whenever you share, you are rewarded by nature,

In your feelings which appear,
To thank you for your behaviour.
The joy of giving,
To you is what nature brings,
Lonely hearts, together in rhythm they sing.

For whatever you share, be it a thought,
Or the things that you have bought.
Your worries and your dreams,
Or your nightmares and your screams.
Your hidden secrets, and some gossips.
Be they your pleasures,
Or your sorrows and your pains,
Be they your tears,
Your embarrassments, your shames.
Or from the dust,
The gathered pieces of your broken heart,
The disgusting smell of an early morning fart,
Or the disappointments that come from an awful start.

On someone's shoulder your head to rest upon,
With arms embracing and forgiving
The wrong that you have done.
A shoulder absorbing your mournful tears of grief,
Your sorrows have found
A channel for their relief.
To share them all,
Whatever they may be,
With friends and strangers,
Or just the family,
When sorrows are shared,
The lighter is the misery,
And so too are your embarrassments,
Your disappointments and your hanky panky.

This is the way, the effect of sharing,
It is nature's way, to display a hand forgiving.

For each person you share with,
Your teardrops keep reducing
Until gone are the pains and the sorrows in your feelings.

But the need to share is not a need only to give.
For you to share, there must be someone to take.
And if you do not take, then no one can ever give.
So your sharing need is, indeed, a give and take.

Consider for a moment just how you feel,
When someone refuses your hand in need.
Or your hand stretched out in gratitude,
Is rejected with an offensive attitude.
You denied the person the rewards in giving,
To see the smile on your face
And enjoy that comforting feeling.
You robbed him the privilege with you to share
And his self-satisfaction
Which was a bit unfair.

You give so often
And more often you take.
You share with your family,
With strangers and your mates.
And you take it for granted,
It is always candid, the way you feel.
Never realising, that it is sometimes compromising,
This human need.
For this you must be aware
That it is important to strike a balance,
To take more than you give
Could cost you your independence.

Your need is to share,
And to share is to give and take,
Both hands must clap,
And together, for goodness sake.

Or your life will be lonely,
Despite all your money,
If you have no mate.
So you'd better hurry and find somebody,
Before it's too late.
And take good care,
For life is to share;
That is your fate,
God be with you
In everything you do,
And in your gives and your takes.

The Folly of Your Ways

Man know thyself. This has been said to you:
Man know thyself.
And so shall it be, more than anything else.
But how much of yourself do you know,
From your head right down to your toe?
From whence you came, and to where do you go?
Why are you here? And for so short a stay,
Is it to prepare for another life
After you have passed away?

Into the family of man you came
More than two thousand years ago.
And upon a tree you have written your name
So that the history of truth shall know.

Man and woman side by side,
Together you live and together you die.
Man and woman throughout the ages,
With a history of events recorded on pages,
Through a changing world of unpredictable changing times,
Many things you have invented
By your inspiring and your ingenious minds.

Two thousand years gone,
And perhaps even many more,
And what have you accomplished?
A great divide of rich and poor.
Out from the darkness of the ages of cannibalism,
Barbarism and savagery,
Through the slimy tunnels of feudalism,

Fascism, exploitations and slavery.
To the bright new frontiers
That seem to be your ultimate goal,
A system called democracy,
With freedom to crimes that incarcerate your soul.

And what is it that you have achieved,
Who dare so boldly to ask?
Your barbarism, and savagery,
Your exploitations and slavery,
Are all now moulded in a different cast
And written into the books of history,
The present to link up with the past.
Is it for guidance, or just remembrance,
Or to be repeated as just another task?

Could it be your folly,
If not, then what is it?
That after two thousand years
You have not yet cured your ills.
And the colours of your gruesome scales
Worsen as they change,
Oh, savage man of yesterday,
Today you are deranged.

With a partner you have mated,
Just as it was done right through the ages.
Nature's way has remained the same,
From a seed implanted, a new life came.
And delivered unto you
Is a new-born babe,
From nature's genetic instructions,
Beautifully it has been made.

And to carry from you a replica,
In some small way or the other.
A child from nature you behold,

With your love and affection, as much as you could.
And sometimes with others you have to share
Each child from your womb of which to take good care.

And within your shelter you protect your children,
Quite often giving one a lot more attention.
You imposed your will upon your kids,
Your life is a model of how they must live.
Instead of their own; hers and his.
You denied them an education
For them to help to pay the bills.
Your possessiveness and your selfishness
Add to their spoils and to their ills.

You taught your children the things that you know,
And passed unto them the folly of your ways.
And it is not until older they grow,
That they realise how foolishly you behave.

You abuse your child sexually,
And you are neither ashamed or sorry.
You disguised yourself as a gentleman in society,
Concealed in you is your lechery.
Taking advantage of the prejudice about,
No one will believe; everyone will doubt,
To think that a child so wilfully will accuse
His or her parents of sexual abuse.
Is it not stupidity and folly on your behalf?
You might as well be but a damned jackass.

The destruction of a child in many ways
Is caused by its parents through the way they behave.
Constant quarrels, assaults and drunkenness,
Lack of attention, absenteism,
Unfaithfulness and aggressiveness;
They are but a few of the causes of the bitterness.

And yet over and over and over again
Repeated in your demeanour you do the same.
And to hide from yourself, you discard the blame,
Or each time you are so sorry, and still it happens again.
It is as if you can't control yourself,
You lose your temper quicker than anything else.
And when that is lost, the suffering it costs.
Just another case for the Inspector Morse.

You can't accept the fact
That your wife earns more than you.
You hate the thoughts of that,
But what can you do?
You can't accept the fact
That your wife is the breadwinner.
That irritates you and makes you feel inferior.
But are you not with her an equal partner,
Then who earns more – why should it matter?
Is this not just the folly of your ways
To despise yourself just because your wife pays.
Man of intelligence, how foolish you can be?
You cut your nose to spite your face,
In a matter of triviality.

That even from a good wife you will depart,
Gone about your own business,
Like a horse that leaves its cart.
And what are your problems
That you can no longer live together?
Romantic candlelight blown out by a stormy weather
When deep down in both of you
There is a reservoir of love,
Just waiting from one to the other to flow,
Whenever you pull the plug.
But yet you allowed pride to tear you apart,
When all that you really wanted
Was to make a fresh start.

So you packed your bags and were gone with the wind,
A few days later, a tug-of-love would begin.
Each parent now loves the child,
As they never did before,
As they take up arms and armour,
In a battle, a tug-of-war.
At your child's mind
You pull and you tug until you dislocate,
Playing your silly game of spite,
In your tug of love and hate.

So another child, cast from side to side,
Becomes insecured and unhappy,
And to be innocently counted as a misfit in society.
With many scars leaving disfigured marks on his mentality,
And all because of your inconsiderate breaking up of the family.

Was it love, hate, pride or your damned folly?
That you could not hold steady your shaky matrimony,
Making the efforts that were really necessary,
To heal the wounds that seemed so bloody.
Instead, a confused child you now have left,
With one parent to do her best.
Adverse persuasions rush right in,
And innocent children, they lose everything.

Now you are divorced from a knave lover,
Whom you once did love, and now it is all over.
So you become acquainted with another partner,
Only to repeat your blunders again,
In love. Hate and divorce; that is the game.

And yet each time you feel that you have found the right partner,
With whom the rest of your life would be spent, both together.

That is exactly what you once said, one to the other.

When your rugged lips get moistened with a kiss,
Your heart beats like a drum, in a romantic bliss.
Your blood warms with your heated passion,
A sleeping serpent is now an erection.
You are in love and you have an enduring romance.
That you dare not take a chance to look any further
Than the distance of your arms,
outstretched with charms,
Embracing one another.

That is when you become a bewildered jackass,
And stumble into love with hopes that it will last.
Hopes of a romantic paradise,
Where nothing else matters in your life.
Until again the odours from your veins begin to smell,
And the magic of your romance loses its spell.
You can't stand each other, so you break apart,
To find another partner and to make a fresh start.

So what do you look for when courting a partner?
Why do you make the same mistakes over and over?
Marrying and divorcing, like it is a game you play,
Learning nothing from your mistakes of yesterday.
Is it because you are a fool,
A pig-headed jackass or a mule
That you can't see any further than your romance,
O silly fool rushing in just to take another chance.
And to cause more suffering and pain,
Broken hearts to be separated once more again.

Many of you as parents you are not fit,
You pass unto your children your disgusting habits.
In societies you flourish only as the weeds,
And your children you disperse them, like unwanted seeds.
Many they never go to school,

Others leave early with an excuse.
Not knowing either how to write or to read,
Vagrants in society is the life they lead.

Most are usually very dull,
And their teachers say, sorry, it is not their fault.
The kids instead of learning, are prone to play,
They will not listen, nor will they obey.
The teachers fail miserably in their duty,
Dull children they dismiss from their responsibility
Because they lack the training, the patience and the will,
They don't have enough time, the ability or the skill.

So dull children always are left behind,
Whilst the bright ones higher and higher they climb.
And they can even go to special selected schools,
Which do not admit you if you are dull
for they called you a fool.
Claiming merit undeservingly,
When they only admit children,
who were bright already.

Such schools have proven absolutely nothing,
Because they do not admit dull children.
It is the dull child who really poses a challenge,
To prove the skill of his teacher's reputable performance.
Geniuses are but another problem,
Their teachers cannot cope with such bright children,
And instead of steering them full speed along,
They are held back and kept just where they don't belong.

All these are follies in the manner of your ways,
To which you become addicted
and duly complacent slaves.
You adopt no commonsense
you learn nothing from your experience,
And as an asshole you live for most of your days.

A child's life is filled with unwarranted difficulties,
Especially when his roots are entangled with those of the weeds.
And because his life is totally dependent,
He becomes subordinate to the ambitions
and to the fears of his parents.
And he is at their persuasions both good and bad;
Decisions are made for him,
which are quite often sad.
And yet no one interferes,
it is none of their business but a family matter.
Hence innocent children are destroyed forever.

You are fed from your environment
where your feet are planted,
And whatever is in the soil,
that is what to you it is granted.
And with many things you are fed,
for your physical and your spiritual,
With superstitions you are possessed,
right from your birth to your burial.

You become a Christian, a Protestant, a Muslim or a Jew,
A Sikh, a Jehovah's Witness, a Buddhist or a Hindu.
And why did you? You haven't got a clue.
It was not of your choice,
but it was imposed upon you.
In one of many faiths
and they all believe in the same God,
But you cannot yet find a common base,
or a single path for us all.
And where is this God in the universe.
Where do you find him?
Is there a church somewhere, in which he lives within?
The learned scientist says, that he does not exist,
There is not such a person, or even such a thing.

And yet as from far up in the heavens and right down to
    earth,
Incomprehensible mysteries controlling objects, life and
    growth.
With everything in order and obeying the rules of nature,
And yet confidently they say that there is no maker.

Is there some folly in learning
where stupidity hides?
To be so very well learned and yet still not wise.
To have the evidence before you, unable to interpret.
Life simply appeared, that is what science said,
But all other things man had to make.

Religion, you have made an important influence in your
    life,
To you it is your faith and a moral daily guide.
It is the path through which
with your God you communicate,
In congregations where you meet
with others who participate.

You go to church and you say
it is to serve God and pray.
But why not do it at home,
or in the fields where you play?
For God is everywhere,
and right here with you,
God is in your kitchen
and in your garage too.
He is in the hospitals among the sick and dying,
And with those locked up in jail,
paying for their sins.
He is with the children in the classrooms,
And with the war-mongers on the battlefields,
You can never escape his presence,
witnessing all your deeds

And listening to your thoughts.
Your secrets you cannot hide.
Unless they are, of course,
taken to your grave when you die.
No need to dress up and go to church,
There's the house of hypocrites tarnished with reproach.
With hearts of stone and songs of praise,
Always shouting up to heaven,
and yet you cannot mend your ways.
Still full of hate and prejudice,
adultery is your whim,
Corruption, vice and wickedness,
always itching under your skin.

He who loves his mother,
need not shower her with praise,
And so it is the will of God.
It is just a matter of doing the things she wants you to do,
And the same it is with God and you.
And whenever you are with a private matter
And you want to feel real close to her,
Then you communicate personally,
and in surroundings privately.
You do not gather all your friends together,
or all of the family.

The same way it is to communicate with God,
The best place is not with a noisy crowd,
All shouting praise extremely loud.
God is never far away,
Nor is he deaf, drunk or asleep.
during the night or during the day.
So there is no need for you to shout,
For He is with you wherever you pray.
Or are you with some doubt?

It is always best to communicate personally

With your God, a friend or the family.
Did not Jesus leave his disciples to go and pray alone?
When many are together,
distractions among you roam.
There is no doubt that you wish to be sincere in your prayer,
But you could be distracted by anything that is there.
Someone's clothes, hat or hairstyle,
The pretty girl, the handsome man sitting nearby
Or an old friend you haven't seen for quite some time.
You are anxious to know if he is doing fine.
Your thoughts wandering but not now in prayer,
They are on the trail of the one at whom you stare.
It is upon her body your thoughts now collide,
And fill you with anxiety, deep down inside.

Some go to church to meet others
and there to socialise and make friends,
But is it a place for a social gathering,
Or a place for your entertainment?
A place for singing and dance, hypocrisy and pretence.
Or a place where you contemplate in fear,
And for your sins you repent.
Be conscious of the fact that God is there,
And from your sins there's no place to run.
Conscious of the fact that God is near,
With a pardon for the sins that you have done.

You go to church quite regularly
but your sinful ways you cannot mend.
Your life is one of duplicity,
and sadly that is how it may end.
You go to church, you say
to learn what is wrong and what is right,
And in God's name it is preached to you
that black is inferior to white.
You must turn the other cheek,
but in a war that will not be right

The enemy you must kill
to damn your soul and save your life.
And pork you should not eat,
The Sabbath is for you to keep.
In confession your sins are forgiven,
Slippery is your pathway to heaven.

What you preached was right yesterday,
is no longer right tomorrow,
But the laws of God are for you to obey,
eternally for you to follow.
The teachings of the church cannot be changed,
If they are the true will of God.
Celibacy, women priests, abortions –
whatever the rules they must remain
If they are commanded from above.
No change in the laws of God – that can never be.
What was a wrong to become a right,
can only be your hypocrisy.
Or what was a right to become a wrong,
reflects the image of your stupidity
And the lack of your understanding since you were born,
And the absurdity of your folly.

In the commandments you are given the righteous laws of
   God
To be obeyed, and for all your days,
Whatever the times, and whatever the cause.
Thou shall not steal, commit adultery,
nor a man must you ever kill,
So it has been written,
and so it is His will.
He did not say to kill in self-defence,
Or to take one's life as a punishment.
Or to kill in disputes declared as war.
That sin will be yours, and that is for sure.

Thou shalt not kill,
so it is written in God's commandment,
And there are no loopholes
or excuses for your involvement.
You love and you fear God,
that is what you say,
But hideous crimes are what you commit
during the hours of every day.
Then you stand or you kneel and bow your head and pray,
Your loathsome crimes and all your sins, mysteriously
  washed away.
But you can be certain, for all your sins,
there will be something you shall have to pay,
Whenever it comes, there is no escape
from justice on your judgement day.

You make religion a dominant influence
in your life of iniquity and cruelty,
Which you execute in the name of a religious authority.
You are a fanatic in your religious beliefs and your fears,
In murderous deeds you wash your hands with blood and
  with tears.
You believe with fear and without a single question,
Many superstitious and fallacious bits of nonsense.
You would not lend yourself to a sensible discussion,
Or listen to a word of religious criticism.

And where is your love, your kindness,
your godliness and your honesty?
When it is never extended beyond your friends and your
  family.
Your charitable ways are only displays of your deception,
It is only those of your faith
whom you embrace with a good intention.
Clearly, folly has become your way in your faith and beliefs,
Hypocritical are your footsteps
Planted upon the sands and the reefs.

But as time arrives and disappears swiftly in the wind,
So too do new attitudes, new styles and ideas end and
   begin.
And some with you a long time they remain,
Generations old and new,
the same things you believe in.
And only because they were passed on to you.
Within the environment where you were born.
Believing in things only because all others do
Your intelligence is worthy of their scorn.

You believe in the superstitions of the past.
Traditions become cultures and forever they last.
But some things are changed,
they moved with the times.
Wrongs become rights and rights become wrongs,
Affecting both punishments and crimes.

Man-made laws are quite often changed,
Magistrates cannot interpret, nor judges explain.
And like a fishing net they are filled with holes.
They can't catch real criminals, or even assholes.

Consider the system by which you are redressed
With laws that don't make sense,
causing despair and distress.
Laws which should have long been changed,
as they no longer suit the times
Because those wrongs of yesterday,
today, they are no longer crimes.

Laws that are stupid, ridiculous and unjust,
And written into the statute books,
where they are numerous.
Imposed upon you to obey, and legally you must,
Or, a price you will pay,
and heavy will be the cost.

The system of justice throughout the ages,
Has left blank spaces for amendments upon its pages.
And what have you got as an ideal judiciary system today?
Two lawyers, a judge and jury,
in a theatrical drama where the losers pay.
Two lawyers, one prosecuting and one defending,
lodged in an intellectual battle of wits,
Supported by witnesses and some experienced courtroom tricks.
The judge referees the battle from where he sits.
And at the end, the jury, who were twelve altogether,
To discuss what they heard, they then retire.
And later they return and announce the winner.

A lawyer can know that his client is guilty,
Yet defend him to the best of his ability.
Because the system says that he is innocent
until he is proven guilty.
Or he may believe that his client is innocent,
And yet persuades him to accept the punishment.
Such is the folly of the system
where criminals often go free,
And upon him who is innocent,
heavy is the penalty.

So what are the functions of the courts?
Where do you look for justice
When the heart of the system depends upon
an intellectual battle of wits,
And the bias and the prejudice of twelve assholes,
Who are either scared, corrupted or revengeful,
And who often have no concern for the cause of justice?
They've made up their minds long before the case is finished.
The guilty they set free and the innocent they punish.

Justice has been squeezed into a legal sandwich

Prepared by lawyers, shared equally by judge and jury.
The innocent is left without any.
That is the feeble truss of the system
that no one cares to mend,
Or to make the necessary adjustments
so that justice can be a friend.
But not only flawed are the laws and the system,
But that which is enforced as a deterrent or a punishment.

Indeed, too often the punishment never suits the crime,
It is either a short stay in jail,
or some ludicrous fine.
And yet the entire system
is by learned men designed,
If that is the best they can achieve,
better they had resigned.

But justice does not only belong
In the courtrooms where it is hoped to be found.
Justice has a rightful place
Wherever it is needed in a case.
It is implemented by most of you
Within the rules of the things you do.
And in your homes, at school and at your work,
The competitions you entered,
and the games you played.
Justice is in the fair decisions,
the ones that are seldom made.

And that is why you live your life in societies unjust,
Some so brutal that free speech is lethal,
there's no one you can trust.
And after more than two thousand years,
Many stained with blood and washed with tears,
You haven't achieved very much.

I am not referring to the material things,

Which have been your inspirations and your ambitious
   aims,
And which you have acquired most successfully,
By the brilliance of your ingenuity
And your highly inspired and motivated discoveries,
Of nature's most secret mysteries.

In that avenue you are profoundly praised,
The knowledge you have acquired made eyebrows raised.
But I am referring to love and generosity,
Kindness and justice, peace and humanity.
I am referring to the values of the soul,
Values to build you a most needed better world.
Values that can bring all nations close together,
In dignity and love and to care for one another.

For more than two thousand years you have lived.
What you have achieved are nations divided
According to religion, colour, culture or language.
Some with a show of a wasteful abundance,
When others have not, even got a pittance.

People who have and those who have not.
People in riches or poverty,
People with daily filled stomachs
and people with stomachs empty.
Some in mansions and many more in shacks,
With squalor and filth in their surroundings,
And destitution the burden upon their backs.
A hell is what they are enduring.
A few are literate and many more illiterate.
Attitudes are developed with little love and more hate.

Yet you fly up to the moon
and the stars way up in the sky,
When right among you here on earth,
millions of starving children die.

You spend billions creating weapons of war,
Wasted and squandered are many billions more.
You are corrupt; you are wicked; you are stupid;
You are obstinate and brutal,
And as a leader of a nation,
the consequences are fatal.

Two thousand years and more,
and what have you acquired?
More wars than ever before,
Millions you have slaughtered.
History you have written,
but nothing you have learned from your mistakes of the
　　past,
It is as though events were only recorded,
to be again repeated.
Now the time has come at last.

You have adopted a system called capitalism,
and that you say is great.
Extreme poverty, a divided society,
millionaires and billionaires,
That is what it creates.
Unemployment and homelessness,
uncertainties with nervousness.
Bankruptcies and miseries,
affecting you and your families.

It is a system governed by market forces,
And institutions of finance set up in high places
Where money matters are on the move daily,
Creating whirlwinds of uncertainty.
And roaring tremors of fear, panic and anxieties,
That unleashed turbulence that rocks the vaults of
　　currencies.

A system of risks and competitions,

Where you lose or gain to your success or your destitution.
A system whereby the rich gets richer,
And at the expense of the poor who becomes poorer.
And governments of nations,
in this diplomatic game they play,
The rich rob the poor in a very deceptive way.
And they wrapped them up in bondage, tightly with heavy loans,
In captivity to stay, with no economy of their own.
Because of the high interest they pay
Nothing is left for development at home.

And to add to their misery corruption successfully thrives,
Especially in high society,
it is an ego; it's the drive.
Loans have been squandered,
and left nations with burdensome debts to pay,
And with little to help them survive,
So as lame ducks always they stay.
And the richer the politicians,
the poorer is their country,
Because their fingers are always busy fiddling in the treasury.
Whilst they stitch up their people permanently in a web of poverty,
And at the same time swelling their foreign bank accounts,
From the revenue of their country.

That is the system called capitalism,
which enslaves you one and all,
Nations, institutions, families and individuals.
And the higher up you are, the harder you fall.
For when you borrow money,
You can end up very sorry,
Trapped in the sewers of financial worries
And left there to struggle with many challenges,
But if you know how you can manage,

You can overcome the difficulties.

But it is often a very desperate struggle,
Even though you may be intelligent, hard working and sensible.
To get out from your rot you often have to fight.
Locked into a battle for long hours at night.
And each step you crawl
To make sure you do not fall.
You grab hold of anything in your sight.
You grab hold of someone's long nose,
A pair of tits, or just their clothes.
Someone's wallet or their lighted cigarette,
Or even on to their balls you grab hold.

Such is the system called capitalism,
mother to riches and poverty,
Which you either inherit, by some means of credit,
Or acquire by your own ability.
It is the system, and none other,
Taken from a page from the book of nature,
The harsh reality of survival of the fittest,
And with consequences that are often the gravest.

Upon your family and your friends you trample,
Upon the old and weak and the disabled.
And upon the sick lying in bed,
Upon them all, both living and dead.
A system that breeds rapacity and selfishness.
Dishonesty, deceit and many vile forms of wickedness.

It is the system accurately described as dog eats dog,
Then it must be a cannibalistic, when also mug eats mug.
And within it are the cheats and exploiters,
Who pay very low wages to their workers.
And they employ child labour.
Hand to mouth wages is what they offer.

Their only concern is making profits.
The welfare of their workers
is none of their business.

A system that denies you medical attention.
If you cannot pay, there is no education.
And so it causes great suffering,
For many to eat they scavenge the dustbins.
With some it is their body they sell,
And even worse, they take drugs as well.
Enslaved in their own hell of prostitution,
Or in an addicted situation.
Strangled by circumstances, and situations not of their
　making,
But by the forces of the system that lie within.

It is a system where money talks
Very loud and clear, for it is the boss.
And most things you do are for yourself and your family,
Hardly do you care a damn about anybody.
And when you have money there's no need to work,
You simply pay for the services of some other bloke
And live from the provisions of society,
Because you need not contribute when you have money.

That is a part of the freedom of capitalism,
To work or not to work – it is your decision.
That is, if you can find work, of course,
Be it as an employee, or as your own boss.
But if you do not work, neither do you eat,
You are trapped in poverty, on a capitalist street.

These are but a few qualms of the system,
Which you so proudly addressed as capitalism.
And in which the masses are stuck
in an odious slime of destitution and muck.

And at the same time, a few are so very rich
that they can stack away millions.
for which they have no use,
But only to lavishly squander
In an exorbitant spending abuse.

And what are the values of such a society,
What are your hopes and what is your priority?
To get rich quick is what it all seems to be.
That even crime pays – so you murder for money
And not only strangers, but also members of your family.

So what do you see as the root of the problems?
No one seems to know,
But they all agree
they made the wrong decisions,
That was quite a few years ago.
And you continue to handle the economy badly.
Recession you say is to blame,
With interest rates changing almost daily,
And confidence washed down the drain.

Many lifestyles become disrupted.
As securities are withdrawn and uprooted.
Never again, is your lifestyle to be the same.
Your good times have now been grounded.
But lucky for you came a rescue,
in the name of socialism,
To soften the pain of the pangs that came
With the trials and tribulations of capitalism.
With a little charity, some caring humanity,
And a great deal of effort to destroy poverty.

A few countries with sound economies,
And wanted to help their poor
To uplift themselves from their financial miseries.
And to a daily meal they can be sure.
So socialism clasped hands with capitalism,

And quite often they squeezed in a fierce opposition.
Because socialism tended to assist the poor,
With handouts that you'd never had before.
Handouts which you began to take for granted,
And became the norm, as it was never intended.
Handouts which made you dependent
Upon state benefits for your requirements.
Handouts which were intended to be helpful,
Became abused and extravagantly wasteful
To the extent where the system nearly collapsed,
As those it intended to help took advantage.
And liberation from poverty became too expensive.

Two thousand years and more,
and what have you achieved?
Capitalism, socialism and communism.
With the last, many were ill at ease.
And yet it could have been the ideal system,
With which you could have been very well pleased.
As it offers you no threat of unemployment
nor other uncertainties.

Free education for all,
and health care a guarantee.
A roof over your head,
is a life-long certainty.
No homelessness or beggars,
child labourers and exploiters,
Those are the capitalist disease.
So what is wrong with communism?
Some of your freedoms are seized.

No millionaires or billionaries,
or a shop for you to keep,
Or any form of business,

when it is your interest that you seek.
What you did was not for yourself,
but for the nation as a whole,
And that is one of the main differences,
Between the capitalist and the communist world.

It is also a system that supports the precept,
that all men are equal,
But that can never be true,
Just have a look at how nature created you.
Some short, some fat, some tall.
Some have brains, others very stupid they remain,
They can't learn anything at all.
So whenever you say,
in your very own way,
that all men are equal,
That can only mean
that it must be seen,
That the same respect is given to all.

Seventy years in practice,
just a fraction of the time
That it took capitalism to be established
And for the people to be so inclined.
And yet you built up a powerful military,
And the arts you had mastered.
But you neglected your country's economy,
And the peoples' needs you disregarded intentionally.

Many factories operated with old machinery,
And the shops were always almost empty
When they should have been filled
and overflowing with plenty
Of goods that were made of a high quality,
With communism thriving in prosperity
Just as it had achieved in the arts and weaponry.
By the disciplined determination of the ruling party.

But wherever you have corruption,
regardless of the system,
All is eventually destroyed.
And that may be why communism died;
corruption was widely employed.

For decades you proscribed capitalism,
And now you sink your feet in its shoes.
To kick at the ball of catastrophic explosions,
A confusion of evils you let loose.
You rid yourself of communism
and the unity of nations combined.
To know not where you are going:
divided you race to climb.

Is it folly, your stupidity, hypocrisy, or what?
That those you once glorified as the heroes of communism,
Today you rejected, discarded, and forgot.
Instead of cleansing the rot that penetrated the system,
You chose to destroy the lot.
And even morals and discipline.
Like a child you destroyed everything,
Not knowing the value of anything,
You left yourself with nothing,
Except, of course, your discontent,
your hunger and your suffering.

Because you thought that the grass was greener on the other
  side,
When all that was needed was to get rid of the weeds,
Right down to the roots until they died.
And then to water and feed,
wherever there was a need,
In keeping communism alive.

Two thousand years and more
and what have you achieved?

For whatever the system, there is always corruption,
And you deceive the people you lead.

Leaders after leaders of nations big and small,
They make false arrests and imprisonments,
and without any rights at all.
Unjustly oppressing their people, with suppressive acts of
   brutality,
And persistently denying them the rights
of a just and democratic society.

But perhaps there are some achievements,
Which in a disguise they may be.
The independence of many nations,
and the ending of human slavery.
But has slavery truly ended?
Before your eyes you can see
The exploitations and the bondage,
in chains tied up are many.

The forming of institutions,
such as the Arab league and the Commonwealth,
And the very many others,
all taking care of themselves.
And the forming of a United Nations,
and human rights to the individual.
But what good are your systems
when those rights are not extended to all?
And what good is a world of institutions,
with leaders brutal and corrupted,
Many who ought to be in prison,
for the crimes that they have committed.
At some time or the other.
And all who gather together,
themselves in a house of scoundrels,
Idiots who did but never,
something honest for anyone else.

And within their house of scoundrels,
There bribery and hypocrisy reign.
And there the bullies influence the rules,
For their selfish political gain.
They flaunt not the cause of justice.
Double standards are common practice.
A house of deceit, liars and thieves.
In the name of humanity, nothing have they achieved.

Just a bunch of assholes leading nations,
Who can't even solve their country's problems.
The poverty, illiteracy, disease and squalor,
Crimes and brutality
and the injustice in their country all over.
And from their shattered economies,
they spend extravagantly on weapons of war.
Destroying their people and the little they have,
Then shamelessly begging for more.
But not to feed their people who daily starve
But to oppress them, and to keep them poor

This is the folly of leaders of nations,
Unfit for their office of authority.
The results are seen in the starvation
And in the actions of their stupidity,
Controlling the lives of millions,
trapped in their poverty and illiteracy.

Others ignore putting their house in order,
To plan coups and assassinations,
where governments are not in their favour.
Interfering in other countries' domestic affairs,
When the policies are not in the interest of theirs.
Ignoring their own problems at home,
Things get so bad, too hot to handle alone.
So then they gather together as proud leaders of nations.
And with their own house in disorder,

they argue about world problems.
And yet nothing do they ever solve peacefully,
Without blood, death and painful misery.

This is because they are just a bunch of fools,
They spend too much on war
Because destruction is what they always choose
Destruction they see as the only way.
The game fools and assholes together they play.
Destruction, the only thing they can agree about,
On everything else, they always have some doubt.

Corrupted leaders of nations big and small.
Corruption in the nooks and in the cracks in the wall.
Corruption in the police and in the judiciary.
And within institutions of high society.
And within the houses of leaders of nations,
Where hypocrites gather to voice their opinions,
With persuasions in debates or in arguments,
And at the same moment destroying their environments.

Terminating both plant and animal life,
Creating a hell where there once was a paradise.
You pollute the air and poison the waters,
And in the sky you destroy the protective layers.
You ignore dangers only to be wise,
After the calamities that left you paralysed.
Although you say that prevention is better than cure,
You prevent not until after disaster knocks down your door.
And for what is the purpose of so much destruction?
The folly of your ways is a dangerous excursion.

Two thousand years and more
and what have you achieved?
A world full of sufferings more than ever before,
And a rat race sponsored by greed.
In what direction are you heading?

To other planets way up in the sky?
When will you act to relieve the sufferings,
And the squalor where millions live and die?
Where lie your ambitions;
what are your priorities?
A paradise right here on earth,
or the conquest of the galaxies?

But problems are not only created by governments.
And neither are they all their responsibility,
But institutions, families and individuals
All stir in the pot of adversity.
You as well as your leaders, can be prudent,
injudicious, brutal and hypocritical,
Since it was from among you that they were chosen
So your attitudes could be identical.
They, like you, are influenced
By the forces within your environment.
And from wherever the soil is poorly,
So it is reflected in the quality of the tree.

You lived your life in an environment,
With the freedoms of a democracy,
And within that jungle you raced along,
To take your place in society.
So many things you learned in your life,
And so many things you believed,
And you remain stupid instead of being wise,
Easily you are deceived.

You are deceived by the politician,
the conman and your doctor.
You are deceived by a friend,
your husband, your wife, your brother.
You are deceived by the priest,
the minister and school teacher,
You are deceived by your solicitor

and the news from the media.
You are deceived by yourself,
From the thoughts that within you dwell.
You are deceived by anybody,
Whether a friend, foe or family.

You believed most of whatever is said,
Your faculty to think quickly disappeared.
You believed in the lies dispensed in advertisements,
And the smooth persuasion of the conmen:
And the sleek tongue of the minister;
The pen and paper of the media;
And the fork tongue of the politician,
He would tell you the truth, but he never can.

So you believe that he is a coward,
the conscientious objector,
Because the politicians told you so,
and nothing else really matters.
You cannot think for yourself,
to realise it is he who is brave.
Because it is easier to follow the crowd
and even to your grave,
Than to stand alone when everyone is against you.
That takes some guts; it is not easy to do.
No one is brave who just follows the crowds,
Whatever the cause, they are but a bunch of cowards.
The more a danger is shared,
the less the danger is feared.
Then everyone follows, without even being scared.

You want to have sex, but you don't want a baby.
Because you are scared, outside matrimony.
You took no precautions to prevent your pregnancy,
You were laid in a gamble, now to wait and see
If it was alright, bad luck or stupidity.
So now you point a finger and accuse;

it is someone else to blame,
When it is you who gets pregnant.
So why leave it up to him?

You cannot commit suicide,
your life is not yours to take.
You cannot commit euthanasia.
On the good Lord you must wait.
But the life within your belly,
you want the right to terminate,
Would that be folly, hypocrisy, or a case of bloodygate?

Over two thousand years you have lived,
And you have made tremendous progress,
Industrially, that is.
Really you have done your best.
You have created a world of beautiful things,
For both your pleasure and your comfort,
Suited to the envious desires of kings.
And despite your intelligence and your ingenuity,
Your brilliance and your understanding and your
    perspicacity,
You seem to lack the wisdom
happily to live together
with your family and your friends
And even with your neighbour.

Broken homes and marriages
have become common practice.
Family values, without excuse,
have become a bankrupt business.
Sodomy and pornography
have become just a way of life –
Man marries man, woman marries woman,
In a bastion of love without husband, without wife.

You have created societies of alcoholics and drug addicts,

And an epidemic so deadly,
with your loathsome sexual permissiveness,
And countless pockets of social misfits
Whom you reject and despise.
And you treat them disrespectfully,
disgustingly and vile,
Condemned to the gutters of society,
To be lynched with stench and ridicule until they die.

And when you are confronted with disputes,
To solve them you resort to a war,
You show no concern for humanity,
And not even for your neighbour next door.
And only because they are of a different colour,
religion, language, or race,
Your attitude towards them
is nothing but a shameful disgrace.

You are no better than primitive man,
A member of the Nazis or the Klu Klux Klan.
Or a member of some secret society,
In conduct so vile and disgusting as a man can ever be.
Even to animals you are cruel and barbaric,
Brutally you slaughter for your pleasure and profit.
And when you do not slaughter,
It is to torture and lame,
To suffer the beast in your barbaric and savage game.
You have no honour, and you have no shame,
Always to point a finger, at someone else for you to blame
For your ills, your madness and your deeds insane.

What is left in the encyclopedia of wickedness
that you have not yet committed
Against man and beast and nature, so barbaric,
that from your records it is omitted?
What is left as a sin forbidden
that you have not yet committed

Against your family, a friend or neighbour –
too vile a crime to be permitted.

Two thousand years and more,
and what have you achieved?
A world so full of plenty,
and yet so many are still in need.
Two-thirds live in poverty;
one third live in luxury.
What is the purpose of that
when all man has the same needs?
Rich and poor together,
it is the same air they breathe,
Equally treated by nature,
they eat, they shit and they bleed.
Together they come and together they go;
nothing they bring and all they leave.
So why not together should you have a go?
Towards the fulfilment of human needs.

Why not a free world market
for all the things you produce?
And for all the people of every nation,
because all are able to afford their use.
What is the point of producing
for so small a world demand?
No wonder you cannot sell all the things you are making,
When only a third of the world enough they are earning
To buy the goods at hand.

Just think for a moment of the tremendous market,
In every country the people can afford it.
In a world of decent living standards,
and morals and discipline too.
Where crime will find no vanguards,
Because values mean something to you.
A world making up a paradise,

because you have willed it to be so,
With no arseholes as leaders
who don't know the right way to go.

This you have accomplished in a single path,
Where men together unite.
And together compete in the feats of their art,
To the world's nations' delight.

In your sporting events all nations play
in high spirits, in jubilation.
And yet sadly it could be, that this jubilee,
would be destroyed by cheats and corruption.
Then what will you have?
Nothing good and all bad,
In your world technically developed.
With you forever prone to greed,
and leaders of nations still corrupt.

And yet right among the thieves, murderers and corrupted
    leaders,
There are many very good people who care,
But too often in your societies,
those are the ones who fear.
And after two thousand years
in so much blood and so much tears
Evil is still the crown you wear.

So what do you intend to do
to make a better world for the future?
Or do you prefer to some other place to go?
To Mars where the grass is greener,
Leaving behind a world unkind,
for generations to live in squalor.
Leaving behind a world unkind,

in destitution where the masses suffer,
Leaving behind a world unkind,
for evil to reign forever.